A Handbook of Ancient Greek Grammatical Terms:
Greek-English and English-Greek

T. Michael W. Halcomb

GlossaHouse

A Handbook of Ancient Greek Grammatical Terms:
Greek-English and English-Greek

GlossaHouse, Inc.
110 Callis Cir.
Wilmore, KY 40390

A Handbook of Ancient Greek Grammatical Terms: Greek-English and English-Greek / edited by T. Michael W. Halcomb

p. cm. — (AGROS Series; Ref.)
Includes bibliographical references.
ISBN-13: 978-0615804095
ISBN-10: 0615804098

Cover Design by Asa Harrison & Klay Harrison.
Text & Book Design by T. Michael W. Halcomb.
The fonts used to create this work are available from www.linguistsoftware.com/lgku.htm.

To Fred Long, a mentor in the Greek language and a friend in whom there is nothing false.

AGROS

Acessible Greek Resources & Online Studies

Series Editors

Fredrick J. Long & T. Michael W. Halcomb

GlossaHouse

πίναξ (Table of Contents)

Introduction to the AGROS Series

The Greek term ἀγρός is a field where seeds are planted and growth occurs. It also can denote a small village or community that forms around such a field. The type of community envisioned here is one that attends to Holy Scripture, particularly one that encourages the use of biblical Greek. Accessible Greek Resources and Online Studies (AGROS) is a tiered curriculum suite featuring innovative readers, grammars, specialized studies, and other exegetical resources to encourage and foster the exegetical use of biblical Greek. The goal of AGROS is to facilitate the creation and publication of innovative and inexpensive print and digital resources for the exposition of Scripture within the context of the global church.

The AGROS curriculum includes five tiers, and each tier is indicated on the book's cover: Tier 1 (Beginning I), Tier 2 (Beginning II), Tier 3 (Intermediate I), Tier 4 (Intermediate II), and Tier 5 (Advanced). In addition, there is a reference collection which contains general reference materials such as lexicons. There are also two resource tracks: Conversational and Translational. Both involve intensive study of morphology, grammar, syntax, and discourse features. The conversational track specifically values the spoken word, and the enhanced learning associated with speaking a language in actual conversation. The translational track values the written word, and encourages analytical study to aide in understanding and translating biblical Greek and other Greek literature. The two resource tracks complement one another and can be pursued independently or together.

Introduction to this Book

By default, students who are interested in ancient Greek must also be interested in ancient texts. This is true even those of us who wish to use Koine Greek in the context of speaking or conversation. It is, after all, from antiquated writings that we learn how Greek was used in the past and, thus, how we can properly use it today. This takes us into the realm of grammar.

This book, as the title suggests, is a book all about ancient Greek grammar. More specifically, this volume is concerned with grammatical terms that were used in antiquity. Having access to these terms allows us to broaden our conversations, especially when speaking in Greek, about the ancient language itself as well as those writings composed in ancient Greek.

Of course, there are many variations of the ancient Greek language. Attic, Ionic, and Koine Greek were but a few dialects used at different periods and in different locations in the ancient world. The terms found in this book are not relegated to one era. What this means is that a term used in Attic might not have been used the same way in Koine and vice versa. Given that there have been so many debates about issues such as dating and authorship among researchers, it was decided that those issues would not be addressed here. Readers are certainly welcome to undertake such research as they desire.

This work is simply meant to function as a user-friendly resource that accomplishes two main objectives: 1) to provide learners with a quick-access guide to ancient Greek grammatical terms; and 2) to assist learners in building their grammatical vocabulary so that they can better engage discourse, whether written or spoken, that occurs in ancient Greek.

How This Book Works

This volume has been strategically arranged into two parts. Both parts contain the same data but are rearranged differently. The first part of the book is alphabetized by Greek grammatical terms. This allows learners to quickly find a Greek word they are looking for. Following the Greek term is one or more simple English glosses, one or more sources in which the Greek term is attested, and lastly a brief example or explanation of the Greek term in English. The second part contains all of the same terms with all of the same data except it is alphabetized, not by Greek terms, but by the English glosses provided.

In sum, there are over 600 Greek grammatical terms listed in this work. As the astute reader will recognize, chief among the ancient sources cited are Apollonius Dyscolus, Dionysius Thrax, and Aristotle. Numerous other primary sources are cited, however, and in each instance I have striven to follow the abbreviation and numbering systems provided by Henry G. Liddell, Robert Scott, et al., *A Greek-English Lexicon* (9th ed.; Oxford: Oxford University Press, 1996). When the work of Liddell, Scott, et al. (LSJ) was either unclear or lacked a citation information, I attempted to use reference details that followed the general consensus among researchers. Readers should also be aware that a number of sources are housed within collections as opposed to standing alone and when this is the case the collection rather than the individual text is cited. You can see this, for example, with references to the *Etymologicum Magnum*. There are also a few instances where an author's name is cited but a title not given (e.g. Eustathius) and at least one instance where no chapter, verse, or line number is provided (e.g. Stephanus Byzantius).

In addition to LSJ, there are several other secondary sources that assisted me in my research that deserve mention here. As many will be aware, *Eleanor Dickey's*

Ancient Greek Scholarship: A Guide to Finding, Reading, and Understanding Scholia, Commentaries, Lexica, and Grammatical Treatises from Their Beginnings to the Byzantine Period (CRS 7; Oxford: Oxford University Press, 2006) is very extensive when it comes to this topic. Although I consulted the list of terms she provides, by no means were all of them adopted in this book. In fact, there are numerous terms in this work that cannot be found in her volume. Further, some of the glosses given to Greek terms that she listed were, in my view, questionable in regards to their use within ancient Greek grammar. Still, Dickey's work is certainly first-rate and is a work I would highly recommend to anyone interested in ancient Greek grammar.

In his work, *Polis: parler le grec ancien comme une langue vivant* (Paris: les Éd. du Cerf, 2009), Christophe Rico offers a list of over 100 Greek grammar terms. A number of Rico's terms are not attested in ancient resources but seem to be reconstructed in reverse based on modern linguistic categories. For example, Rico's construction ἡ κεφαλαία πρότασις (Main Proposition/Clause) is not found anywhere in ancient Greek literature. While this label makes sense and may even be non-problematic to use, because it is not attested it ancient literature, it and other similar reconstructions were not included here.

A much earlier work that I consulted was William Frost's *Alpha: A Greek Primer: Introductory to Xenophon* (Boston, Mass.: Allyn and Bacon, 1889). Frost gives only a couple of pages of terms and many of those can also be found here. There were a number of terms that Frost used (for example, ὁσημέραι), however, which were either irrelevant, unattested, or problematically defined which were not included here. Finally, about two weeks before sending this work to print, I was introduced to R. Dean Anderson Jr.'s *Glossary of Greek Rhetorical Terms Connected to Methods of Argumentation, Figures and Tropes From Anaximenes to Quintilian* (CBET 24; Peeters: Leuven, 2000). While that volume contains a number of terms also included here, as the title suggests, its focus is quite different. Even so, I would highly recommend Anderson's work as it is quite handy, well-structured, and full of helpful ancient Greek rhetorical terms.

In the present volume, I have attempted to use only terms attested in ancient Greek literature. I have not used every term related to or attested in ancient grammar; but then again that was not the goal of this work. Instead, I hope that the words offered within this resource will provide a solid foundation for learners. What distinguishes this handbook from other works such as those already mentioned is that it offers primary source citations as well as examples and explanations in English. This prevents readers from having to consult any number of other works to understand the grammatical concept under discussion.

In closing, I am grateful for the inclusion of this resource in the AGROS series being published by GlossaHouse. Thanks also to Fred Long, to whom this book is dedicated, for his sharp eye and helpful comments in working through the initial draft. I look forward to the many excellent resources that, alongside this, will populate the AGROS Curriculum Suite. I would also like to thank my wife for her partnership and support over the duration of this project. It is my hope that this work will spur on many learners, researchers, and teachers who desire to learn and know ancient Greek as well as ancient Greek grammar.

Easter, 2013
T. Michael W. Halcomb

Part 1

Greek - English

α

ἀβαρβάριστος, ον - Non-barbaric (*Lex. Vind.*) *Lexicon Vindobonense* 294
>Proper and intelligible language or speech.

ἄγμα, τό - Nasal (velar) (Prisc., *Inst.*) Priscianus, *Institutes* 1.39
>A letter spoken that allows air to escape through the nose, for example "m" or "n."

ἀγράμματος, ον - Illiterate, inarticulate (Pl., *Ti.*) Plato, *Timaeus* 23a
>Unable to read, write, or speak.

ἄδεια, ἡ - Poetic license (Him., *Or.*) Himerius, *Orations* 1.1; (A.D., *Pron.*) Apollonius Dyscolus, *On Pronouns* 38.3, 69.19
>Any instance when a speaker or writer disrupts the expected order of speech or grammar to draw further attention to what is being said.

ἀδιάπταιστος, ον - Uninflected (*EM*) *Etymologicum Magnum / Great Etymological Lexicon* 643.47
>Having no inflections. In Greek, the endings of many proper names do not change from case to case.

ἀδιάπτωτος, ον - Uninflected (*EM*) *Etymologicum Magnum / Great Etymological Lexicon* 643.47
>Having no inflections. In Greek, the endings of many proper names do not change from case to case.

ἀδιάστατος, ον - Inseparable (syllable) (A.D., *Pron.*) Apollonius Dyscolus, *On Pronouns* 86.21

Having the characteristic of syllables such as "ea" in the word "conceal." As an inseparable syllable these vowels cannot be separated.

ἀδιάστολος, ον - Undistinguished (A.D., *Pron.*) Apollonius Dyscolus, *On Pronouns* 11.26
When a word's case or gender may not be defined or recognizable.

ἀδιαφορέω - Not in agreement (A.D., *Pron.*) Apollonius Dyscolus, *On Pronouns* 45.22, 68.15
For example, when a subject and the verb do not agree with one another in a sentence.

ἀδιαχώριστος, ον - Undistinguished (*EM*) *Etymologicum Magnum* / *Great Etymological Lexicon* 538.34
When a word's case or gender may not be defined or recognizable.

ἀδιπλασίαστος, ον - Non-doubled (Eust.) Eustathius, 781.15
A single letter instead of a pair of letters. For example, a non-reduplicated augment or stem.

ἀδόκιμος, ον - Unapproved, unconvincing (Ph., *Bel.*) Philo Mechanicus, *Excerpts* 76.47
The use of ungrammatical speech or forms, or when an argument or speech is not convincing.

ἄθροισις, ἡ - Group, collection (Porph., *Abst.*) Porphyrius Tyrius, *On Abstinence* 1.29
A group of words or texts.

ἀθροιστικός, ἡ, όν - Collective (w/nouns), copulative (w/conjunctions) (A.D., *Synt.*, *Conj.*) Apollonius Dyscolus, *On Syntax* 42.24, *On Conjunctions* 230.20

A collective term such as "nouns" or "eyes," etc.

αἰτιατική, ἡ - Accusative (D.T., *Ars gram*.) Dionysius Thrax, *Art of Grammar*, 636.6; (A.D., *Pron*.) Apollonius Dyscolus, *On Pronouns* 11.9
> A grammatical case that denotes the "object" of either a transitive verb or a preposition.

αἰτιατικός, ἡ, όν - Accusative (D.T., *Ars gram*.) Dionysius Thrax, *Art of Grammar* 636.6; (A.D., *Pron*.) Apollonius Dyscolus, *On Pronouns* 11.9
> Having the characteristic of being a grammatical case that denotes the "object" of either a transitive verb or a preposition.

αἰτιολογικός, ἡ, όν - Causal (conjunction) (A.D., *Conj., Adv*.) Apollonius Dyscolus, *On Conjunctions* 231.4, *On Adverbs* 200.2
> A conjunction that express a "cause." For example, "because."

ἀιτιολογικός, ἡ, όν - Causal (A.D., *Conj., Adv*.) Apollonius Dyscolus, *On Conjunctions* 231.4, *On Adverbs* 200.2
> Expressive of the relationship between two actions or events. For example, cause and effect.

αἰτιώδης, ες - Causal (Chrysipp., *Stoic*.) Chrysippus, *Stoicism* 2.70
> Expressive of the relationship between two actions or events. For example, cause and effect.

ἀκαταλληλία, ἡ - Not in agreement (A.D., *Synt*.) Apollonius Dyscolus, *On Syntax* 167.1
> For example, when a subject and the verb do not agree with one another in a sentence.

ἀκατάλληλος, ον - Ungrammatical, not in agreement (A.D.,
Synt.) Apollonius Dyscolus, *On Syntax* 30.5
> When a word is used incorrectly, for example, a slang
> term or solecism. In English, "a'int" is typically
> understood as "improper."

ἀκλισία, ἡ - Indeclinability (A.D., *Pron.*) Apollonius Dyscolus,
On Pronouns 12.4
> Incapable of being inflected.

ἄκλιτος, ον - Indeclinable (A.D., *Synt.*) Apollonius Dyscolus,
On Syntax 30.10
> Lacking grammatical inflection. A word stays the same
> regardless of case. For example, in Greek the name
> Μιχαηλ (Michael).

ἀκολουθέω - To follow (logically) (Pl., *Phd.*) Plato, *Phaedo*
1499a1007b; (Hermog. Id.) Hermogenes, *On Ideas* 400e
> When, in a conditional sentence the protasis ("if")
> is followed by the apodosis ("then"), giving us an
> "if/then" statement.

ἀκολουθία, ἡ - Agreement, analogy (D.H., *Amm.*) Dionysius
Halicarnassensis, *Letter to Ammaeum* 2.2; (A.D., *Pron.*)
Apollonius Dyscolus, *On Pronouns* 2.24
> The subject and verb agree in person, number, and
> gender.

ἀκόλουθος, ον - Analogous, analogical (A.D., *Pron.*)
Apollonius Dyscolus, *On Pronouns* 11.21
> When one thing is similar or comparable to another thing.

ἀκυριολέκτητος, ον - Incorrectly (used) (Hermog., *Meth.*)
Hermogenes, *On The Method of Effective Speech* 3
> Having the characterstic of being used incorrectly. For

example, a slang term or solecism. In English, "a'int" is typically understood as "improper."

ἀκυρολέκτητος, ον - Incorrectly (used) (Hermog., *Meth.*) Hermogenes, *On The Method of Effective Speech* 3
> Having the characterstic of being used incorrectly. For example, a slang term or solecism. In English, "a'int" is typically understood as "improper."

ἀκυρολεξία, ἡ - Incorrect phrasing (Eust.) Eustathius, 1770
> To improperly use a phrase or figure of speech, to mispronounce.

ἀκυρολογέω - To speak incorrectly (*Lex. Vind.*) *Lexicon Vindobonense* 3.19
> To improperly use a phrase or figure of speech, to mispronounce.

ἀκυρολογία, ἡ - Incorrect phrasing (D.H., *Lys.*) Dionysius Halicarnassensis, *On Lysias* 4
> To improperly use a phrase or figure of speech, to mispronounce.

ἄκυρος, ον - Improperly used words or phrases (Cic., *Fam.*) Cicero, *Letters to Friends* 16.17.1
> When a word is used incorrectly, for example, a slang term or solecism. In English, "a'int" is typically understood as "improper."

ἄληκτος, ον - No ending (Demetr. Lac., *Herc.*) Demetrius Lacon, *Herculaneum Papyri* 1061.7
> A sentence or writing that seems very long or without ending.

ἀλλοπαθής, ές - Non-reflexive (A.D., *Pron.*, *Synt.*) Apollonius Dyscolus, *On Pronouns* 44.17, *On Syntax* 175.13
> When the action of a subject is not placed or focused back upon itself.

ἀλλοπαθῶς - Transitively (Eust.) Eustathius, 920.27
> Characteristic of verbs that take a direct object.

ἄλογος, ον - Unrhythmical (syllables) (D.H., *Comp.*) Dionysius Halicarnassensis, *On Word Order* 20
> Unequal in measures of syllables.

ἀλφάβητος, ὁ - Alphabet (*An. Bachm.* or *AB*) *Anecdota Graeca / Greek Anecdotes* 181
> In English, a group of ordered letters such as A, B, C (in Greek, Α, Β, Γ).

ἀμερής, ές - Indivisible, inseparable (Arist., *APo.*) Aristotle, *Posterior Analytics* 100b2
> Having the characteristic of syllables such as "ea" in the word "conceal." As an inseparable syllable these vowels cannot be separated.

ἀμετάβατος, η, ον - Intransitive (A.D., *Pron.*) Apollonius Dyscolus, *On Pronouns* 44.12
> Characteristic of verbs that do not take a direct object.

ἀμετάβλητος, ον - Uninflected (A.D., *Synt.*) Apollonius Dyscolus, *On Syntax* 322.26
> Words that have no inflections. In Greek, the endings of many proper names do not change from case to case.

ἀμετάθετος, ον - Uninflected (A.D., *Synt.*) Apollonius Dyscolus, *On Syntax* 322.1
> Words that have no inflections. In Greek, the endings of

many proper names do not change from case to case.

ἀμφιβολία, ἡ - Ambigous word, ambiguity (A.D., *Synt.*)
Apollonius Dsyscolus, *On Syntax* 311.10
> A word that often has more than one sense or meaning
> and is open to various interpretations.

ἀναβιβάζω - To retract an accent (throw an accent backward)
(A.D., *Pron., Synt.*) Apollonius Dyscolus, *On Pronouns* 49.15,
On Syntax, 308.10
> When an accent is thrown (leftward) back toward the
> front of a word.

ἀναγινώσκω - To read, interpret (Pi., *O.*) Pindar, *Olympian
Odes* 10.1
> Usually the act of decoding and understanding written
> characters or symbols.

ἀναγραμματισμός, ὁ - Transposed letter used to help form
another word (Eust.) Eustathius 45
> An anagram. For example, where the letters in the word
> "great" can be inverted to spell "retag."

ἀνάγω - To form, derive, refer to (A.D., *Synt.*) Apollonius
Dyscolus, *On Syntax* 266.13
> To form a word or sentence from various grammatical
> parts.

ἀναδίπλωσις, ἡ - Reduplication (Trypho, *Fr.*) Trypho,
Fragments 12
> When the stem or root of a word is repeated. For
> example, in Greek when the verb λανθάνω becomes
> λέληθεν in the perfect tense. (The λ is doubled.)

ἀνάδοσις, ἡ - Retraction (of an accent) (*EM*) *Etymologicum Magnum / Great Etymological Lexicon* 549.30
> When an accent is thrown (leftward) back toward the front of a word.

ἀνακόλουθος, ον, ία - Irregular, anomalous (A.D., *Pron.*) Apollonius Dyscolus, *On Pronouns* 66.1
> A deviation from standard usage or meaning.

ἀνάκρισις, ἡ - Question, inquiry (Pl., *Phdr.*) Plato, *Phaedrus* 277e
> An expression used to ask for data or information about someone or something.

ἀναλογητικός, ή, όν - Analogous, analogical (A.D., *Conj.*) Apollonius Dyscolus, *On Conjunctions* 241.14
> When one thing is similar or comparable to another thing.

ἀναλογία, ἡ - Analogy (A.D., *Synt.*) Apollonius Dyscolus, *On Syntax* 36.23
> A comparison of one thing to another.

ἀνάλογος, ον – Proportionate (Arist., *EN.*) Aristotle, *Nichomachaen Ethics* 1158a35
> Balanced or even. For example, syllables in a word or words in a sentence.

ἀνάλυσις, ἡ - Analysis (Arist., *EN.*) Aristotle, *Nichomachean Ethics* 1112b23
> Parsing a complex idea into smaller portions so as to understand it with more clarity.

ἀναμερίζω - To parse (break into parts) (A.D., *Synt.*) Apollonius Dyscolus, *On Syntax* 114.3
> To break down a word or idea into smaller portions so as

to understand it with more clarity.

ἀναμφίβολος, ον - Unambiguous (Ascl., *Tact.*) Asclepiodotus, *Tacitus* 12.11
>Incapable of being interpreted or understood more than one way.

ἀνανταπόδοτος, ον - Not having an apodosis (Ar., *Pl.*) Aristophanes, *Plutus* 469
>A conditional sentence that lacks the "then" part of an "if/then" statement.

ἀνάπαυσις, ἡ - Pause, cadence, period (Hermog., *Id.*) Hermogenes, *On Ideas* 1.1
>A temporary stop or a repetitive rhythm often marked with the symbol (.).

ἀναπέμπω - To retract, throw an accent backward (Hdn., *Gr.*) Herodianus, *Prosody* (*Herodiani Technici reliquiae*) 278
>When an accent is thrown (leftward) back toward the front of a word.

ἀναπόδοτος, ον - Not having an apodosis (Ar., *Av.*) Aristophanes, *Aves* 7
>A conditional sentence that lacks the "then" part of an "if/then" statement.

ἀναπολέω - To repeat (Pi., *N.*) Pindar, *Nemean Odes* 7.104
>To say or write more than once.

ἀναπόλησις, ἡ - Repetition (A.D., *Synt.*) Apollonius Dyscolus, *On Syntax* 29.10
>To be said or written more than once.

ἀνάπτυξις, ἡ - Explanation (Arist., *Rh.Al.*) Aristotle, *Rhetorica ad Alexandrum* 1.1a
>Answer or statement given to describe or clarify a matter.

ἀναστρέφω - To invert order (e.g. words or accents) (Demetr., *Eloc.*) Demetrius Phalereus, *On Style* 11
>To place the verb before the subject.

ἀναστροφή, ἡ - Anastrophe, inversion (A.D., *Synt.*) Apollonius Dyscolus, *On Syntax* 308.15
>To place the verb before the subject.

ἀνάτασις, ἡ - Raised pitch/voice (with an acute accent) (D.T., *Ars gram.*) Dionysius Thrax, *Art of Grammar* 620.1
>The raising of pitch when pronouncing a word with an acute accent.

ἀνατρεπτικός, ή, όν - Refuted, privative (Hermog., *Meth.*) Hermogenes, *On The Method of Effective Speech* 10
>Something that has been proven erroneous or wrong.

ἀνατρέπω - To refute (Ar., *Nu.*) Aristophanes, *Clouds* 901
>To prove something erroneous or wrong.

ἀναυξησία, ἡ - Omitted augment (Greg.Cor., *Trop.*) Gregorius Corinthius, *On Tropes* 180
>In Greek when a past tense augment is omitted or left off of the front of a verb.

ἀναφέρω - To repeat (Pl., *Ti.*) Plato, *Timaeus* 26a
>To say or write more than once.

ἀναφορά, ἡ - Anaphora, repetition (Longin.) Longinus 20.1
>To say or write more than once.

ἀναφορικὴ ἀντωνυμία, ἡ - Relative pronoun (Theodos., *Can.*)
Theodosius, *Canons (On Grammar)* 19.9
>   A pronoun that can function as a subject, object, or
>   possessive pronoun (e.g. who, that, whose).

ἀναφορικός, ή, όν - Relative (A.D., *Pron.*) Apollonius
Dyscolus, *On Pronouns* 5.20
>   Having the characteristic of a pronoun that can function as
>   a subject, object, or possessive pronoun (e.g. who, that,
>   whose).

ἀναφώνημα, τό - Interjection (Heph., *Poëm.*) Hephaestio, *On
Poems* 5.3
>   "Oh!" "No!" "Sorry!", for example.

ἀνέγκλιτος, ον - Unencliticized (A.D., *Synt.*) Apollonius
Dyscolus, *On Syntax* 136.7
>   Characteristic of not receiving the effects of an enclitic.

ἀνεκφώνητος, ον - Unpronounced (letters) (*EM*) *Etymologicum
Magnum / Great Etymological Lexicon* 203.7
>   For example, in Greek, the iota subscript.

ἀνομοιογενής, ές - Of a different gender (S., *Ant.*) Sophocles,
Antigone 74
>   Not of the same gender (e.g. masculine, feminine, neuter).

ἀνομοιοκατάληκτος, ον - Of a different ending (A.D., *Synt.*)
Apollonius Dyscolus, *On Syntax* 167.25
>   Not of the same case ending (e.g. nominative, genitive.,
>   etc.).

ἀνομοιόπτωτος, ον - Of a different case (Eust.) Eustathius
1228.62
>   Not of the same case (e.g. nominative, genitive, etc.).

ἀντανάκλαστος, ον - Reciprocal, reflexive (Prisc., *Inst.*)
Priscianus, *Institutes* 11.1
> Characteristic of subjects in a sentence that are able to
> direct the action of the verb back upon themselves (e.g.
> "myself").

ἀντανακλάω - To be reflexive (A.D., *Synt.*, *Pron.*) Apollonius
Dyscolus, *On Syntax* 175.12, *On Pronouns* 28.3
> When the subjects of a sentence are able to direct the
> action of the verb back upon themselves (e.g. "myself").

ἀνταποδοτικός, ή, όν - Correlative (A.D., *Adv.*, *Conj.*)
Apollonius Dyscolus, *On Adverbs* 158.24, *On Conjunctions*
237.9
> One word that is connected to or has a relatioship with
> another word, i.e. "connective."

ἀντιδιαστέλλω - To be definite (A.D., *Synt.*) Apollonius
Dyscolus, *On Syntax* 37.7
> The be the opposite of indefinite or ambiguous; often
> marked by the definite article "the."

ἀντίθεσις, ή - Antithesis (Arist., *Rhet.*) Aristotle, *Rhetoric*
1410a22
> An opposing or contrasting idea that is parallel to another
> idea. For example, black/white, wrong/right, etc.

ἀντιμετάληψις, ή - Interchanged form (A.D., *Adv.*) Apollonius
Dyscolus, *On Adverbs* 155.1
> When one word can be spelled two different ways; or
> like a chiasm, where one block of information
> interchanges with another.

ἀντιπαραβάλλω - To compare (Pl., *Hp.Mi.*) Plato, *Hippias Minor* 369c
> To show similar traits between two items.

ἀντιπαράθεσις, ἡ - Contrast, comparison (A.D., *Synt.*)
Apollonius Dyscolus, *On Syntax* 49.21
> Different or similar traits between two items.

ἀντιπεπονθώς, υἶα, ός - Reciprocal, reflexive (*Stoic.*)
Stoicorum Veterum Fragmenta / Old Stoic Fragments 2.59
> Characteristic of subjects in a sentence that are able to
> direct the action of the verb back upon themselves (e.g.
> "myself").

ἀντιστοιχέω - To correspond to (letters) (*EM*) *Etymologicum Magnum / Great Etymological Lexicon* 443.17
> When aspirated or unaspirated sounds correspond to
> certain letters. For example, the hissing sound
> corresponds to the letter sigma.

ἀντιστρέφω - To invert (A.D., *Synt.*) Apollonius Dyscolus, *On Syntax* 180.16
> To turn inward, upside down, or in reverse order.

ἀντιστροφή, ἡ - Antistrophe, inversion of letters, or repetition
of a sound or word (usually at the end of a line or sentence)
(Eust.) Eustathius 945.60; (EM) *Etymologicum Magnum / Great Etymological Lexicon* 424.8
> Interchanging stanzas in a Greek choral ode.

ἀντίστροφος, ον - Antistrophic (Arist., *Pr.*) Aristotle, *Problems* 918b27
> Characteristic of interchanging stanzas in a Greek choral
> ode.

ἀντίφρασις, ἡ - Antiphrasis (word used in a sense opposite of its common meaning) (Trypho, *Trop.*) Trypho, *On Tropes* 2.15
>   When a word is used to convey its opposite meaning, often ironically. For instance, in English the "driveway" is where cars park, not drive.

ἀντωνυμία, ἡ - Pronoun, antonym (A.D., *Pron.*) Apollonius Dyscolus, *On Pronouns* 2.1
>   A word that substitutes for another word, which often prevents repetition. For example, words such as "he," "she," "it," etc.

ἀντωνυμικός, ἡ, όν - Pronomial (A.D., *Synt.*) Apollonius Dyscolus, *On Syntax* 156.7
>   Characteristic of a pronoun.

ἀνυπόκριτος, ὁ - Punctuation mark (D.T., *Ars gram.*) Dionysius Thrax, *Art of Grammar* 24h
>   Symbols or markings that denote the organization and intentions of a sentence.

ἀξιωματικός, ἡ, όν - Declarative, axiomatic (*Stoic.*) *Stoicorum Veterum Fragmenta / Old Stoic Fragments* 2.61
>   Having the characteristic of a statement (as opposed to a command or question) or a true saying.

ἀόριστος, ὁ - Aorist (tense) (A.D., *Synt.*) Apollonius Dyscolus, *On Syntax* 276.5
>   A verb form that denotes the past tense without suggesting whether what took place in the past was habitual or has ongoing effects.

ἀπαρέμφατος, ὁ - Infinitive (A.D., *Synt.*) Apollonius Dyscolus, *On Syntax* 76.16, 2226.20
>   A verb form that acts and often functions like a

substantive.

ἀποδεικτικός, ή, όν - Demonstrative (Arist., *APo.*) Aristotle, *Posterior Analytics* 74b10
> Characterisic of words such as pronouns and adjectives that point to specific things often making them definite. They are also referred to as "determiners."

ἀπόδοσις, ή - Apodosis (D.H., *Th.*) Dionysius Halicarnassensis, *On Thucydides* 52
> The "then" part of an "if/then" conditional statement.

ἀποδοτικός, ή, όν - Concerned with the apodosis (*EM*) *Etymologicum Magnum* / *Great Etymological Lexicon* 763.8
> Having to do with the "then" part of an "if/then" statement.

ἀποθετικός, ή, όν - Deponent (*An. Bachm.*) *Anecdota Graeca* / *Greek Anecdotes* 2.303, 2.304
> Verbs that are active in their meaning but take a passive or middle form.

ἀποκοπή, ή - Elision, apocope (A.D., *Synt.*) Apollonius Dyscolus, *On Syntax* 6.11
> In Greek when ἀλλά is followed by a word that begins with a vowel and becomes ἀλλ' (thus the final alpha is removed).

ἀπορηματικός, ή, όν - Negative particle (A.D., *Conj.*) Apollonius Dyscolus, *On Conjunctions* 258.15
> An element or word of speech that negates another word or sentence, such as οὐκ in Greek.

ἀποστροφή, ή - Apostrophe, elision (A.D., *Pron.*) Apollonius Dyscolus, *On Pronouns* 46.1

In Greek when ἀλλά is followed by a word that begins with a vowel and becomes ἀλλ' (thus the final alpha is removed).

ἀπότασις, ἡ - Referent (A.D., *Synt.*) Apollonius Dyscolus, *On Syntax* 35.38
> The person or thing to which an expression refers.

ἀποτείνω - To refer to (Luc., *Nigr.*) Lucianus, *Nigrinus* 13
> To speak of a person, place, thing, idea, etc.

ἀποφαντικός, ἡ, όν - Categorical, declarative (Arist., *Int.*) Aristotle, *On Interpretation* 17a8
> Having the characteristics of being put in a category or of a statement (as opposed to a command or question).

ἀποφατικός, ἡ, όν - Negative particle (A.D., *Synt.*) Apollonius Dyscolus, *On Syntax* 245.24
> An element or word of speech that negates another word or sentence, such as οὐκ in Greek.

ἀπρόσωπος, ον - Impersonal (verb) (Phld., *Lib.*) Philodemus, *On Bold Speech* 290
> Characteristic of a verb that has no specific subject. For example, in the sentence "It is clear." there is no specific or determinate subject.

ἄπτωτος, ον - Indeclinable (A.D., *Synt.*) Apollonius Dyscolus, *On Syntax* 176.5
> Characteristic of words having no inflections; in Greek the endings of many proper names do not change from case to case.

ἀρθρικός, ἡ, όν - Articular (A.D., *Synt.*) Apollonius Dyscolus, *On Syntax* 6.5

Having the characteristics of the article or accompanying the article.

ἄρθρον, τό - Article (Arist., *Rh.Al.*) Aristotle, *Rhetorica ad Alexandrum* 1435a35
The word "the."

ἀριθημτικός, ή, όν - Numerical (Arist., *EN.*) Aristotle, *Nichomachean Ethics* 1106a35
Having to do with number(s).

ἀριθμός, ό - Number (Secund., *Sent.*) Secundus, *Sentences* (Or: *Opinions*) 4
A mathematical symbol used to express an amount or to count. In grammar it refers to singularity and plurality.

ἀρκτικός, ή, όν - Initial (A.D., *Synt.*) Apollonius Dyscolus, *On Syntax* 28.19
To be first or at the front of.

ἄρνησις, ή - Negation (D.T., *Ars gram.*) Dionysius Thrax, *Art of Grammar*, 642.3; (Lesb.) Lesbonax, 26
The act of making a word or statement negative.

ἀρρενικός, ή, όν - Masculine (Ph., *Leg.*) Philo, *On the Sacred Laws of Allegory* 1.294
A grammatical category whose words are often related to "male" persons or things but which also contains many words that, in terms of sexual gender, are arbitrary.

ἀρσενικός, ή, όν - Masculine (D.T., *Ars gram.*) Dionysius Thrax, *Art of Grammar*, 634.17
A grammatical category whose words are often related to "male" persons or things but which also contains many words that, in terms of sexual gender, are arbitrary.

ἄρσην, ὁ (ἡ) - Masculine (Ar., *Nu.*) Aristophanes, *Clouds* 682
A grammatical category whose words are often related to
"male" persons or things but which also contains many
words that, in terms of sexual gender, are arbitrary.

ἀσαφής, ές - Inarticulate (Arist., *Aud.*) Aristotle, *On Sounds* (Or:
On Things Heard) 801b21
The inability to speak properly.

ἄσκησις, ἡ - Exercise, practice (Hp., *VM*) Hippocrates, *On
Ancient Medicine* 4
An exam or quiz.

ἀστιγής, ές - Without punctuation (St.Byz.) Stephanus
Byzantius (# N/A)
When a writing or speech lacks punctuation.

ἀστιξία, ἡ - Unpunctuated writing (*An. Ox.*) Anecdota Graeca /
Greek Anecdotes 4.51
When a writing or speech lacks punctuation.

ἀσυναίρετος, ον - Uncontracted (Eust) Eustathius 50.36
When a word form takes an affix or suffix without
contracting or morphing.

ἀσυνάλειπτος, ον - Lacking synaloepha (i.e. merging of two
syllables into one) (Hdn., *Gr.*) Herodianus, *Prosody* (*Herodiani
Technici reliquiae*) 2.912
When two syllables are not merged into one but remain
distinct.

ἀσύναρθρος, ον - Indefinite article (A.D., *Synt.*) Apollonius
Dyscolus, *On Syntax* 101.5
Lacking an article. In English this may be represented by

"a" or "an."

ἀσύντακτος, ον - Irregular, ungrammatical (Choerob., in Theod.) Choerboscus, cited in Theodorus 18H (see *Anthologia Graeca*)
> Having the characteristic of not being grammatically normative, sound, or correct.

ἀσυνταξία, ἡ - Ungrammatical, grammar error (A.D., *Pron.*, *Synt.*) Apollonius Dyscolus, *On Pronouns* 14.3, *On Syntax* 304.24
> A misspelling or some similar grammatical problem.

ἀσύστατος, ον - Irregular, inadmissible (A.D., *Pron.*) Apollonius Dyscolus, *On Pronouns* 55.11
> Having the characteristic of not being grammatically normative, sound, or correct.

ἄτονος, ον - Unaccented (Emp., *Sphaer.*) Empedocles, *Sphere* 1.141
> A word lacking an accent or change in pitch.

αὐθυπότακτος, ον - Aorist subjunctive (Hdn., *Epim.*) Herodianus, *Partitions* 278
> The subjunctive form of the aorist is suggestive of something that will happen if the proper conditions are met or fulfilled.

αὔξησις, ἡ - Augment (*EM*) *Etymologicum Magnum* / *Great Etymological Lexicon* 338.47
> The vowel prefixed to the front of Greek words which denotes "past tense" or "past time."

αὐτοπαθής, ές - Reflexive (A.D., *Pron.*) Apollonius Dyscolus, *On Pronouns* 44.11

Characteristic of subjects in a sentence that are able to
direct the action of the verb back upon themselves (e.g.
"myself").

αὐτοτελής, ές - Intransitive, self-ending (A.D., *Synt.*)
Apollonius Dyscolus, *On Syntax* 116.11
> A verb that has or takes no direct object.

αὐτουδέτερος, ον - Neuter (*An. Bachm.*) Anecdota Graeca /
Greek Anecdotes 2.302
> Characteristic of words often related to "neuter" or
> "sexless" things; words that, in terms of sexual gender,
> are arbitrary.

ἀφαιρέω - To elide, remove letters or words, to subtract (Pl.,
Plt..) Plato, *Politics* 262d
> In Greek when ἀλλά is followed by a word that begins
> with a vowel and becomes ἀλλ' (thus the final alpha is
> removed).

ἄφθογγον, τό - Mute, voiceless (Pl., *Philb.*) Plato, *Philebus*
18c, (Pl., *Cra.*) Cratylus 424c
> A letter that causes a vocal stop and prevents further
> airflow (e.g. "t" or "d").

ἄφωνα (γράμματα) - Consonants (Pl., *Cra.*) Plato, *Cratylus*
393e
> A letter that is not a vowel (e.g. d" or "n").

ἀχώριστος, ον - Inseparable (Arist., *EN.*) Aristotle,
Nichomachaen Ethics 1102a30
> The "ea" syllable in the word "conceal" is an inseparable
> syllable, i.e. these vowels cannot be separated.

βαθμός, ὁ - Degree (interval in rhythm) (Iamb., *VP.*)
Iamblichus, *Life of Pythagorus* 26.120
>   For example, the length between one syllable, word, or
>   beat and the next.

βαρβαρίζω - To use barbaric speech (i.e. unGreek speech) (Pl.,
Tht.) Plato, *Theaetetus* 175d
>   In the ancient world, this was often understood as the act
>   of using non-Greek speech or words.

βαρβαρισμός, ὁ - Barbarism, foreign word (A.D., *Synt.*)
Apollonius Dyscolus, *On Syntax* 198.7
>   In the ancient world, barbaric speech was often
>   understood as non-Greek speech. A barbarism could also
>   denote a misspelled, mispronounced or foreign (non-
>   Greek) word.

βαρυντικός, ή, όν - Retracted (accent) (*EM*) *Etymologicum
Magnum / Great Etymological Lexicon* 763.8
>   When an accent is thrown (leftward) back toward the
>   front of a word.

βαρύνω - To pronounce without accents (A.D., *Synt.*) Apollonius
Dyscolus, *On Syntax* 120.4
>   To say a word without inflection, pitch, or accent change,
>   that is, to say the word in a monotone manner.

βαρύς, ὁ - Grave (accent) (Pl., *Cra.*) Plato, *Cratylus* 399b
>   A mark (`) used to denote a pitch drop on a syllable.

βαρύτης, ἡ - Grave (accent) (Arist., *Po.*) Aristotle, *Poetics* 1456b33

>A mark (`) used to denote a pitch drop on a syllable.

βαρύτονος, ον - Barytone (not oxytone) (A.D., *Pron.*) Apollonius Dyscolus, *On Pronouns* 35.25

>A word not having the acute accent on the last syllable.

βιβλιακός, ἡ, όν - Bookish (related to books) (Porph., *Abst.*) Porphyrius Tyrius, *On Abstinence*, 47

>Having the characteristic of being related to books.

βιβλίον, τό - Small book, scroll (LXX, *1 Ma.*) *1 Maccabees* 12.9

>A small collection of writings.

βίβλος, ἡ - Book, scroll (Phil., *Abr.*) Philo, *About Abraham* 1.9

>A collection of writings.

βουστροφηδόν - Writing from right to left & left to right alternatively (Paus.) Pausanias 5.17.6

>A ancient writing pattern in which one line is written from right to left, the next from left to right, etc.

βραχεῖα συλλαβή - Short syllable (D.T., *Ars gram.*) Dionysius Thrax, *Art of Grammar* 631

>A syllable containing a short vowel.

βραχύνω - To shorten (Pl., *Per.*) Plutarch, *Pericles* 4

>To modify a long syllable into a short one.

βραχύς, εῖα, ύ - Short syllable or vowel (D.T., *Ars gram.*) Dionysius Thrax, *Art of Grammar* 631

>A word containing a short syllable or short vowel such as "bug" in English.

γενική, ἡ - Genitive (D.T., *Ars gram.*) Dionysius Thrax, *Art of Grammar* 636
> A grammatical category that usually indicates possession but can also indicate source, measure, etc.

γενικός, ή, όν - Genitive (D.T., *Ars gram.*) Dionysius Thrax, *Art of Grammar* 636
> Characteristic of a grammatical category that usually indicates possession but can also indicate source, measure, etc.

γένος, τό - Gender (Arist., *Rhet.*) Aristotle, *Rhetoric* 1407b7
> Linguistic category that identifies whether a word is masculine, feminine, or neuter.

γλῶσσα, ἡ (γλῶττα) - Language, dialect, foreign word (Demetr., *Eloc.*) Demetrius Phalereus, *On Style* 177
> A system of speech and communication used to talk.

γράμμα, τό - Letter (A., *Pr.*) Aeschylus, *Prometheus* 460
> A symbol or character used to represent speech sounds.

γράμματα, τά - Alphabet, records (Pl., *Cra.*) Plato, *Cratylus* 390e
> In English, a group of ordered letters such as A, B, C (in Greek, Α, Β, Γ).

γραμματεύς, ὁ - Scribe, scholar (A., *Fr.*) Aeschylus, *Fragments* 358
> Someone who practices the art of writing or composition.

γραμματικεύομαι - To be a grammarian (Pall.) Palladius (see *Anthologia Graeca*) AP9.169
> Someone who practices the art and rules of grammar.

γραμματική, ἡ - Grammar (Pl., *Cra.*) Plato, *Cratylus* 431e
> The system and structure of a language.

γραμματικός, ὁ - Grammarian (Clem.Al., *Strom.*) Clement of Alexandria, *Stromata* (Or: *Miscellanies*) 1.16.79
> Someone who practices the art and rules of grammar.

γραμματιστής, ὁ - Grammar expert (X., *Smp.*) Xenophon, *Symposium* 4.17
> Someone who has mastered the art and rules of grammar.

γραφή, ἡ - Writing, scripture (Pl., *Phdr.*) Plato, *Phaedrus* 274b
> A text or an object containing composed words usually believed to be sacred (such as a book or scroll).

δασύ, τό - Rough (breathing) (A.D., *Synt.*) Apollonius Dyscolus, *On Syntax* 319.20

>Often understood as the "h" sound pronounced particularly before a vowel or vowel pair (diphthong).

δασύνω - To aspirate (A.D., *Pron.*) Apollonius Dyscolus, *On Pronouns* 12.21

>Often understood as the act of pronouncing the "h" sound particularly before a vowel or vowel pair (diphthong).

δασύς, εῖα, ύ - Aspirated (D.T., *Ars gram.*) Dionysius Thrax, *Art of Grammar* 631.22

>Often characteristic of a word or syllable having the "h" sound particularly before a vowel or vowel pair (diphthong).

δεικτικὴ ἀντωνυμία, ἡ - Demonstrative pronoun (A.D., *Pron.*) Apollonius Dyscolus, *On Pronouns* 9.17

>Words such as pronouns and adjectives that point to specific things often making them definite. They are also referred to as "determiners."

δεικτικός, ή, όν - Demonstrative (A.D., *Pron.*) Apollonius Dyscolus, *On Pronouns* 5.19

>Characterisic of words such as pronouns and adjectives that point to specific things often making them definite. They are also referred to as "determiners."

δεῖξις, ἡ - Demonstrative (referent) (A.D., *Pron.*) Apollonius Dyscolus, *On Pronouns* 9.8

>Words such as pronouns and adjectives that point to

specific things often making them definite. They are
also referred to as "determiners."

διάβασις, ἡ - Transitivity (A.D., *Synt.*) Apollonius Dyscolus,
On Syntax 202.7
> Referring to a verb that is able to transfer action to the
> direct object.

διαβατικός, ἡ, όν - Transitive (A.D., *Synt.*) Apollonius
Dyscolus, *On Syntax* 43.18
> Characteristic of verbs that take a direct object.

διαβιβαστικός, ἡ, όν - Transitive (A.D., *Synt.*) Apollonius
Dyscolus, *On Syntax* 298.15
> Characteristic of verbs that take a direct object.

διάθεσις, ἡ - Voice (A.D., *Synt.*) Apollonius Dyscolus, *On
Syntax* 210.19
> A grammatical category descriptive of the relationship
> between the state or action of the verb and the subject.

διαίρεσις, ἡ - Resolution (of a diphthong into two syllables or
one word into two words) (A.D., *Pron.*) Apollonius Dyscolus,
On Pronouns 87.2
> When a pair of vowels are not merged into one syllable
> but remain distinct.

διαιρετικός, ἡ, όν - Disjunctive (*Stoic.*) *Stoicorum Veterum
Fragmenta / Old Stoic Fragments* 2.87
> A word that expresses a disconnect or contrast between
> words, thoughts, ideas, etc.

διάλεκτος, ἡ - Language, dialect (Hdn., *Gr.*) Herodianus,
Prosody (*Herodiani Technici reliquiae*) 2.932
> A system of speech and communication used to talk.

διάλληλος, ον - Interchangeable (A.D., *Adv.*) Apollonius
Dyscolus, *On Adverbs* 126.2
>   When one block of information interchanges with
>   another. For example, in a chiasm.

διάλυσις, ἡ - analyzed element, solution to a problem (A.D.,
Synt.) Apollonius Dyscolus, *On Syntax* 243.11
>   Having been examined carefully and methodically, often
>   leading to the resolution of a problem.

διάνοια, ἡ - Thought, meaning (Pl., *Sph.*) Plato, *Sophists* 263d
>   A mental or intellectual result or product of thinking.

διαπίπτω - To be in error (Arr., *Epict.*) Arrianus, *Writings on
Epictetus* 2.22.36
>   To make a mistake spelling, writing, or speaking.

διασαφητικός, ἡ, όν - Declarative, explanatory, affirmative
(A.D., *Conj.*) Apollonius Dyscolus, *On Conjunctions* 221.23
>   Having the characteristic of a statement (as opposed to a
>   command or question) or a true saying.

διάστασις, ἡ - Separation of vowel sounds or words (A.D.,
Pron.) Apollonius Dyscolus, *On Pronouns* 87.4
>   An instance of epenthesis, i.e. an instance where a
>   consonant may be inserted to separate vowels that do not
>   belong together.

διαστέλλω - To make definite, pronounce (A.D., *Synt.*)
Apollonius Dyscolus, *On Syntax* 37.7
>   To make the opposite of indefinite or ambiguous, which is
>   often achieved by using the definite article "the"; or to
>   pronounce a word.

διαστολή, ἡ - Comma, pause (D.T., *Ars gram.*) Dionysius
Thrax, *Art of Grammar* 629

>A mark or action signifying a brief suspension of speech
or writing.

δίγαμμα, τό - Digamma (A.D., *Pron.*) Apollonius Dyscolus, *On
Pronouns* 76.32

>The ancient Greek letter or symbol similar to the English
"ϝ" that had a sound similar to "v."

διγενής, ές - Of two genders, of doubtful gender (Eust.)
Eustathius 150.27

>A word that is ambiguous in gender.

διήγημα, τό - Story, tale (LXX, *Ezek.*) *Ezekiel* 17.2

>An account of a series of events.

διηγματικός, ή, όν - Descriptive, narrative-like (Arist., *Po.*)
Aristotle, *Poetics* 1459a17, 1459b36

>Having the characteristics of a detailed account or an
account in general.

διόρθωσις, ἡ - Correction (Arist., *SE.*) Aristotle, *Sophistic
Refutations* 176b34

>That which replaces a mistake.

διπλασιασμός, ὁ - Reduplication (A.D., *Synt.*) Apollonius
Dyscolus, *On Syntax* 323.6

>When the stem or root of a word is repeated. For
example, in Greek when the verb λανθάνω becomes
λέληθεν in the perfect tense. (The λ is doubled.)

διπλόος, η, ον - Compound, composite (Arist., *Po.*) Aristotle,
Poetics 1459a9

>Parts of a word or sentence joined to form a whole.

διπλοῦς, ῆ, οῦν - Compound, composite (Arist., *Po.*) Aristotle, *Poetics* 1459a9

 Parts of a word or sentence joined to form a whole.

διπρόσωπος, ον - Dual (A.D., *Pron.*) Apollonius Dyscolus, *On Pronouns* 17.1, 110.24

 Having the characteristics of being a pair.

δίπτωτος, ον - Having two cases or endings (A.D., *Pron.*) Apollonius Dyscolus, *On Pronouns* 91.7

 A word that is characteristic of having two case endings.

δισύλλαβος, ον - Disyllabic (A.D., *Pron.*) Apollonius Dyscolus, *On Pronouns* 49.14

 Having the characteristic of having two syllables.

διφθογγίζω - To construct/write a diphthong (Eust.) Eustathius 1571.29

 The act of writing a vowel pair in Greek such as ου.

δίφθογγον, τό - Diphthong (Hdn., *Epim.*) Herodianus, *Partitions* 245

 A pair of vowels that form one syllable.

δίφθογγος, ἡ - Diphthong (A.D., *Adv.*) Apollonius Dyscolus, *On Adverbs* 128.8

 A pair of vowels that form one syllable.

δοτική, ἡ - Dative (A.D., *Synt.*) Apollonius Dyscolus, *On Syntax* 28.23

 The case that often denotes the indirect object in a sentence.

δοτικός, ἡ, όν - Dative (A.D., *Synt.*) Apollonius Dyscolus, *On Syntax* 28.23

Characteristic of the case that often denotes the indirect object in a sentence.

δραστήριος, ον - Active (D.H., *Th.*) Dionysius Halicarnassensis, *On Thucydides* 24
Characteristic of the state of being or action related to the subject.

δραστικός, ή, όν - Active (*Stoic.*) *Stoicorum Veterum Fragmenta* / *Old Stoic Fragments* 2.133, 2.134
Characteristic of the state of being or action related to the subject.

δυϊκός, ή, όν - Dual (A.D., *Pron.*) Apollonius Dyscolus, *On Pronouns* 10.28
Having the characteristics of being a pair.

δύναμαι - To mean (Ar., *Fr.*) Aristophanes, *Fragments* 691
To signify, denote, or convey some type of thought, concept, idea, etc.

δύναμις, ή - Meaning (Pl., *Cra.*) Plato, *Cratylus* 394b
The thought, concept, idea, etc., that the subject intends to send or express to recipients.

δυνητικός, ή, όν - Potential (of particles) (A.D., *Synt.*) Apollonius Dyscolus, *On Syntax* 10.28
Words that express possibility as opposed to actuality.

δυσεκφώνητος, ον - Difficult to say/pronounce (Eust.) Eustathius 76.33
A word that is not easy to pronounce or say.

δυσήκοος, ον - Unpleasant sounding (Demetr., *Eloc.*) Demetrius Phalereus, *On Style* 48

The opposite of euphonic; the use of barbaric words, speech, or sounds.

δυσκίνητος, ον - Clumsiness (of language) (Pl., *R.*) Plato, *Republic* 503d
> Something said or written in such a way that is grammatically questionable.

δύσκλιτος, ον - Difficult to inflect (*EM*) *Etymologicum Magnum / Great Etymological Lexicon* 763.8
> Characteristic of words having no inflections; in Greek the endings of many proper names do not change from case to case.

δύσφωνος, ον - Unpleasant sounding (Demetr., *Eloc.*) Demetrius Phalereus, *On Style* 69
> The opposite of euphonic; the use of barbaric words, speech, or sounds.

ἐγερτικός, ή, όν - Enclitic (*An. Bachm.* or *AB*) *Anecdota Graeca / Greek Anecdotes* 1147

> Having the characteristic of being an enclitic, that is, a second word that is usually pronounced as though it is connected to the first word. In Greek, this often occurs with personal pronouns that follow a word.

ἔγκλιμα, τό - Inflected form (A.D., *Synt.*) Apollonius Dyscolus, *On Syntax* 83.2

> A word that has been altered by the addition of affixes (i.e. prefixes, infixes, and suffixes).

ἐγκλίνω - To inflect, pronounce as an enclitic, or pronounce with the grave accent (A.D., *Synt.*) Apollonius Dyscolus, *On Syntax* 120.10

> To change the form of a word in order to express a specific grammatical concept, idea, function, etc.

ἔγκλισις, ή - Mood, mode, change of acute to grave accent, inflection (A.D., *Synt.*, *Pron.*, *Adv.*; Dexipp., in *Cat.*) Apollonius Dyscolus, *On Syntax* 248.14, *On Pronouns* 8.7, *On Adverbs* 169.23; Dexippus in *Commentary on Aristotle's Categories* 33.8

> A grammatical category that denotes the reality of what the verb expresses (e.g. actuality, potentiality, etc.).

ἐγκλιτικός, ή, όν - Enclitic (A.D., *Synt.*) Apollonius Dyscolus, *On Syntax* 222.22

> Having the characteristic of being an enclitic, that is, a second word that is usually pronounced as though it is connected to the first word. In Greek, this often occurs with personal pronouns that follow a word.

εἰδικός, ή, όν - Specific (A.D., *Synt.*) Apollonius Dyscolus, *On Syntax* 230.11
>Having the characteristic of belonging to a particular category.

εἶδος, τό - Style, form, something written (*EM*) *Etymologicum Magnum / Great Etymological Lexicon* 763.8
>A particular aspect, detail, or pattern related to a speech or composition.

εἰκάζω - To compare (Arist., *EN.*) Aristotle, *Nichomachean Ethics* 1106b30
>To show similar traits between two items.

εἰσαγωγή, ή - Introduction (D.H., *Amm.*) Dionysius Halicarnassensis, *Letter to Ammaeum* 2.1
>The frontal or opening material of a writing or speech.

ἐκβολή, ή - Digression, close of a verse (Philostr., *Her.*; Eust.) Philostratus, *The Heroic* 19.14; Eustathius 900.24
>An abrupt change of subject in the middle of a speech or writing.

ἐκθηλύνω - To feminize (*EM*) *Etymologicum Magnum / Great Etymological Lexicon* 473.35
>To make something have the characteristics of being feminine.

ἐκθλίβω - To elide, drop out (A.D., *Conj.*) Apollonius Dyscolus, *On Conjunctions* 228.17
>In Greek when ἀλλά is followed by a word that begins with a vowel and becomes ἀλλ' (thus the final alpha is removed).

ἐκκόπτω - Gendered words marked by different endings (A.D., *Synt.*) Apollonius Dyscolus, *On Syntax* 104.23

> When substantives express different gender based on their endings.

ἐκλειπτικός, ή, όν - Elliptical (Pall., in *Hp.*) Palladius, in *Hippocrates* 2.145d

> Having the characteristics of ellipsis.

ἐκτείνω - To lengthen or augment (A.D., *Pron.*) Apollonius Dyscolus, *On Pronouns* 27.2

> To lengthen the sound of a vowel often through augmentation, that is, the addition of letters (esp. vowels) on to the front of a root or stem.

ἐκφέρω - To pronounce (D.H., *Comp.*) Dionysius Halicarnassensis, *On Word Order* 15

> To enunciate or speak a sound.

ἐκφονέω - To Pronounce (D.H., *Comp.*) Dionysius Halicarnassensis, *On Word Order* 14

> To enunciate or speak a sound.

ἐκφορά, ή - Pronunciation (D.H., *Comp.*) Dionysius Halicarnassensis, *On Word Order* 14

> An enunciated or spoken sound.

ἔλλειψις, ή - Ellipse, ellipsis (A.D., *Synt.*) Apollonius Dyscolus, *On Syntax* 117.19

> A grammatical feature that represents an omission. In English, the markings "…" denote ellipsis.

ἐμπαθής, ές - Modified, inflected (A.D., *Synt.*) Apollonius Dyscolus, *On Syntax* 47.16

> To make partial changes to a word or word group which

often convey extra details or meaning.

ἐμφαίνω - To indicate (D.S.) Diodorus Siculus 1.87
> To denote or point out.

ἔμφασις, ἡ - Emphasis (Demetr., *Eloc.*) Demetrius Phalereus,
On Style 130
> Extra stress or significance upon a word or idea.

ἐμφατικός, ἡ, όν - Emphatic (Demetr., *Eloc.*) Demetrius
Phalereus, *On Style* 68
> Having the characteristics of expressing emphasis.

ἐναντιωματικός, ἡ, όν - Adversative (A.D., *Conj.*) Apollonius
Dyscolus, *On Conjunctions* 251.3
> Having the characteristics of expressing opposition or
> contrast.

ἐναρκτικός, ἡ, όν - Inchoative (*Lex.Vind.*) *Vindobonense
Lexicon* 19.3 (ε)
> Denoting the beginning of verb's action.

ἐνεργητικός, ἡ, όν - Active (A.D., *Adv.*) Apollonius Dyscolus,
On Adverbs 161.18
> Characteristic of the state of being or action related to the
> subject.

ἐνέργεια, ἡ - Active (voice) (A.D., *Synt.*) Apollonius Dyscolus,
On Syntax 9.9
> Denotes the state of being or action related to the subject.

ἐνεστώς, ὁ - Present (tense) (A.D., *Pron.*) Apollonius Dyscolus,
On Pronouns 58.7
> Expresses action or state of being at the time of speaking.

ἔνθεσις, ἡ - Insertion (Pl., *Cra.*) Plato, *Cratylus* 426c
> That which has been placed inside of something (e.g. a word) or in between something (e.g. letters or words).

ἐνικός, ἡ, όν - Singular (A.D., *Pron.*) Apollonius Dyscolus, *On Pronouns* 12.11
> Having the characteristic of being single.

ἔννοια, ἡ - Definition (Hermog., *Prog.*) Hermogenes, *Progymnasmata* 6
> The meaning of a thought, concept, word, idea, etc.

ἐντολή, ἡ - Command (NT, *1 Ep. Cor.*) *1 Corinthians* 7.19
> An order given by an authoritative figure.

ἐξαλλαγή, ἡ - Variant, variation (Procl., *Inst.*) Proclus, *Theological Institutes* 162, 175
> A form of something that differs in one or more respects from a form of something else (that is usually similar).

ἐξέτασις, ἡ - Examination, exam (Pl., *Ap.*) Plato, *Apology* 22e
> For example, a test or quiz. Also a detailed review of someone or something.

ἐξηγέομαι - To interpret (Pl., *Cra.*) Plato, *Cratylus* 407a
> To carefully draw meaning out of and explain a text or speech.

ἐξηγητής, ὁ - Exegete, interpreter, commentator (Pl., *Euthphr.*) Plato, *Euthyphro* 4d, 9a
> Someone who practices the acts of exegesis and interpretation.

ἐξήγησις, ἡ - Exegesis, explanation, interpretation (Pl., *Lg.*) Plato, *Laws* 631a

The act of drawing meaning out of a text or speech and carefully interpreting its meaning.

ἐπεξηγηματικός, ή, όν - Epexegetical (Pl., *Phd.*) Plato, *Phaedo* 64d
Extra or additional words used that did not need to be used.

ἐπίθετον, τό (ἐπιθετικόν) - Adjective (A.D., *Synt.*) Apollonius Dyscolus, *On Syntax* 41.15
A grammatical category consisting of words that modify nouns.

ἐπίθετος, ον - Adjectival (D.T., *Ars gram.*) Dionysius Thrax, *Art of Grammar* 636.9
Having the characteristics of being an adjective.

ἐπίρρημα, τό - Adverb (D.H., *Comp.*) Dionysius Halicarnassensis, *On Word Order* 2
A modifier that qualifies verbs, other adverbs, and adjectives.

ἐπισημασία, ή - Mark, note (Phld., *Rh.*) Philodemus, *Rhetoric* 1.12
A word or symbol used to draw attention to particular thoughts, ideas, or words.

ἐπισταλτικός, ή, όν - Dative (D.T., *Ars gram.*) Dionysius Thrax, *Art of Grammar* 636.6
Characteristic of the case that often denotes the indirect object in a sentence.

ἐπιστολή, ή - Epistle, letter (NT, *2 Ep. Cor.*) *2 Corinthians* 3.2
A literary genre usually denoting letters but sometimes poems.

ἐπιταγματικός, ή, όν - Postpositive, subsidiary (of the pronoun αὐτός) (A.D., *Pron.*) Apollonius Dyscolus, *On Pronouns* 45.12
> A word that cannot come first in a sentence or an affix that cannot come first in a word.

ἐπίτασις, ή - Emphasis (A.D., *Conj.*) Apollonius Dyscolus, *On Conjunctions* 223.4
> The special importance or significance assigned to a word, idea, concept, etc.

ἐπιτατικός, ή, όν - Intensified, intensive (A.D., *Conj.*) Apollonius Dyscolus, *On Conjunctions* 223.4
> Having the characteristic of a word that is an intensifier or has been affected by an intensifier, that is, a word that has been more greatly emphasized.

ἐπιτατικός, τό - Intensive (Theoc., Sch.) Theocritus, *Scholia* (Or: *Scholastic Sayings*) OC632
> An adjective, particle, or adverb that helps emphasize a thought, concept, idea, etc.

ἐπιτείνω - To raise in pitch, to intensify (Phld., *Po.*) Philodemus, *On Poems* 2.18
> Having the characteristic of being spoken with great acuteness.

ἐπιφορητικός, ή, όν - Inferential, illative (A.D., *Conj.*) Apollonius Dyscolus, *On Conjunctions* 258.16
> Having the characteristics of an inference that has been drawn.

ἐπιφώνημα, τό - Interjection (*An. Bachm.* or *AB*) Anecdota Graeca / Greek Anecdotes 100
> An emphatic remark, such as an exclamation, that often

begins, ends, or interrupts speech.

ἐπιφώνησις, ἡ - Address (Phld., *Lib.*) Philodemus, *On Bold Speech* 140

    An act or form of speaking to another person.

ἑρμηνεία, ἡ - Translation, interpretation (Pl., *R.*) Plato, *Republic* 524b

    That which is rendered from one language into another or that which is explained in detail.

ἑρμηνευτικός, ἡ, όν - Interpretive, explanatory (Pl., *Plt..*) Plato, *Politics* 260d

    Having the characteristics of being explained in detail.

ἐρώτημα, τό - Question (Pl., *Prt.*) Plato, *Protagorus* 336d

    An expression used to ask for data or information about someone or something.

ἐρωτηματικός, ἡ, όν - Interrogatory (Hermog., *Prog.*) Hermogenes, *Progymnasmata* 3

    Having the characteristics of being a question.

ἐτυμηγορία, ἡ - Etymology (See: ἐτυμολογία, ἡ)

    Either the origins or a word or the study of the origins of a word.

ἐτυμολογέω - To etymologize (trace a word's origins) (*EM*) *Etymologicum Magnum / Great Etymological Lexicon* 220.37

    The act of tracing the origins of a word.

ἐτυμολογία, ἡ - Etymology (A.D., *Adv.*) Apollonius Dyscolus, *On Adverbs* 153.13

    Either the origins or a word or the study of the origins of a word.

ἐτυμολογικός, ή, όν – Etymological (*EM*) *Etymologicum
Magnum / Great Etymological Lexicon* 700.24
> Having the characteristics of etymology.

εὐγραμματία, ή - Calligraphy (Gal., *Capt.*) Galen, *On
Language and Ambiguity* 14.587
> A style or form of writing that is often described as
> visually pleasing and artistic.

εὐκτικός, ή, όν - Optative (A.D., *Synt.*) Apollonius Dyscolus,
On Syntax 248.6
> A grammatical mode or mood used to indicate a desire,
> wish or hope.

εὐμάλακτος, ον - Liquid consonant (*EM*) *Etymologicum
Magnum / Great Etymological Lexicon* 700.24
> A letter spoken without friction and which can be
> prolonged, such as "r" or "l" in English.

εὐσύντακτος, ον - Syntactially well-formed (Eust.) Eustathius
66.36
> Having the characteristic of proper syntax (sentence
> construction).

εὐφωνία, ή - Euphony (Demetr., *Eloc.*) Demetrius Phalereus, *On
Style* 68
> The pleasantness or agreeableness of sound.

εὔφωνος, ον - Euphonic, euphonious (Demetr., *Eloc.*) Demetrius
Phalereus, *On Style* 70
> Having the characteristic of sounding good or pleasing.

εὐχή, ή - Prayer, wish, vow (Hom, *Od.*) Homer, *Odyssey* 10.526
> An activity used to express oneself with a deity.

ἡ μέση στιγμή - Semicolon, colon (D.T., *Ars gram.*) Dionysius Thrax, *Art of Grammar* 314.11
> A punctuation mark that indicates a short break or pause in a writing.

ἡμίφωνον, τό - Semi-vowel (D.T., *Ars gram.*) Dionysius Thrax, *Art of Grammar* 631.16
> The sound of a vowel or a vowel-like sound that functions as a consonant. In English, for example, the "y" in "yell" is said to function like a consonant.

ἡμίφωνος, ον - Half-pronounced (Aristaenet.) Aristaenetus 1.10
> Having the characteristic of not being fully pronounced.

ἦχος, ὁ - Sound, breath, echo (A.D., *Synt.*) Apollonius Dyscolus, *On Syntax* 290.24
> Audible noises heard with the ear.

θέμα, τό - Base form, root, radical (A.D., *Pron.*) Apollonius Dyscolus, *On Pronouns* 11.21

> The part of a word that does not change and to which affixes are added.

θεματίζω - To determine arbitrarily (a meaning or gender of a word) (S.E., *M.*) Sextus Empiricus, *Against Mathematicians* 1.149, 1.152, 8.202

> Attempting to determine a gender for a non-gendered object.

θεματικόν, τό - Principal parts (A.D., *Adv.*) Apollonius Dyscolus, *On Adverbs* 121.5

> The forms of a verb from which its inflected forms can be realized.

θέσις, ἡ - Form, long syllable (D.T., *Ars gram.*) Dionysius Thrax, *Art of Grammar* 632.30

> In English the syllable "ee" in the word "feet" is long. In the Greek word λόγου the syllable "ου" is long.

θηλυκός, ή, όν - Feminine (A.D., *Synt.*) Apollonius Dyscolus, *On Syntax* 222.6

> Having the characteristics of being feminine.

θηλύνω - To feminize (Vett.Val.) Vettius Valens 76.6

> To make something have the characteristics of being feminine.

θηλυπρεπής, ές - Feminine (Dam., *Pr.*) Damascius, *On Principles* 192

Having the characteristics of being feminine.

θηλύς, εῖα, ύ - Feminine (Arist., *Po.*) Aristotle, *Poetics* 1458a10
Having the characteristics of being feminine.

ι

ἰδίως - Properly, appropriate (Dam., *Pr.*) Damascius, *On Principles* 40

> Having the characteristics of being proper, right, or correct.

ἰδιώτης, ὁ - One unskilled in grammar or writing (Pl., *Phdr.*) Plato, *Phaedrus* 258d

> Someone who cannot read, write, or speak accurately or articulately.

ἰδιωτικός, ή, όν - Unskilled (Arist., *Po.*) Aristotle, *Poetics* 1458a21

> Characteristic of someone or something that lacks a specific set of skills or qualities.

ἰδιωτισμός, ὁ - Vulgar language (Phld., *Po.*) Philodemus, *On Poems* 2.71

> The improper or inappropriate use of language or the improper and inappropriate language itself.

ἰσάριθμος, α, ον - Agreement in number (A.D., *Synt.*) Apollonius Dyscolus, *On Syntax* 170.13

> Characteristic of an instance when a subject is singular and its matching pronoun is also singular.

ἰσοσύλλαβος, ον - Isosyllabic (having balanced number of syllables) (A.D., *Pron.*) Apollonius Dyscolus, *On Pronouns* 11.8

> Characteristic of an instance when one the amount of syllables in one word are the same as the amount of syllables in another word.

ἰσόχρονος, ον - Agreement in length/time units (A.D., *Synt.*)
Apollonius Dyscolus, *On Syntax* 272.23
Characteristic of a one line of a poem contains the same
amount of syllables as another line of a poem.

ἱστορικός, ή, όν - Historical (e.g. present tense verb) (Arist.,
Po.) Aristotle, *Poetics* 1451b1
Having to do with or concerning history. The use of a
present tense verb to describe a state or event related to
the past.

ἰωτογραφέω - To write an iota (Ar., *V.*) Aristophanes, *Vespae
Scholia* 926
To write the Greek letter iota (ι).

𝓚

καιρικός, ή, όν - Temporal (Eust.) Eustathius 17.3
> Having the characteristic of being related to time or tense.

κακοσυνταξία, ή - Bad grammar/syntax (Eust.) Eustathius 210.29
> A writing or speech, for example, that contains and/or is charactersitic of grammatical or syntactical errors.

κακόφωνος, ον - Unpleasant sounding (Arist., *Aud.*) Aristotle, *On Sounds* (Or: *On Things Heard*) 802b23
> The opposite of euphonic; the use of barbaric words, speech, or sounds.

κάλαμος, ὁ - Writing utensil (NT, 3 Ep. Jo.) *3 John* 13
> A quill, pen, etc.

καλλιφωνέω - To pronounce or speak pleasantly/beautifully (Phld., *Rh.*) Philodemus, *Rhetoric* 1.176
> To utilize euphony in speech.

καλλιφωνία, ή - Euphony (D.T., *Ars gram.*) Dionysius Thrax, *Art of Grammar* 675.14
> The pleasantness or agreeableness of sound.

κανονίζω - To conjugate (Opp., *Sch.*) Oppianus Anazarbensis, *Scholia* H.1.259
> To give different forms of a word in light of grammatical categories such as tense, voice, mood, person, and number.

κανόνισμα, τό - Grammar rule (Eust.) Eustathius 439.26

A principle or law governing the use of grammar.

κανών, ὁ - Rule, paradigm (A.D., *Adv.*) Apollonius Dyscolus, *On Adverbs* 141.25
> The common or usual pattern of how words and/or other grammatical entities form and function.

κατάλογος, ὁ - Catalog, list (Pl., *Tht.*) Plato, *Theaetetus* 175a
> A list of items such as people, goods, places, etc.

καταφατικός, ή, όν - Emphatic (A.D., *Pron.*) Apollonius Dyscolus, *On Pronouns* 49.11
> Having the characteristics of expressing emphasis.

κατάχρησις, ἡ - Catachresis (mixed metaphor) (D.H., *Comp.*) Dionysius Halicarnassensis, *On Word Order* 3
> The purposeful misuse of a word often for dramatic effect.

κατηγορέω - To identify or signify the predicate (Arist., *Top.*) Aristotle, *Topics* 140b37
> To point out, for example, that in the sentence "Michael sings." the predicate is "sings."

κατηγόρημα, τό - Direct Object (Arist., *Int.*) Aristotle, *On Interpretation* 20b32
> A noun (or noun phrase) that receives the action of the verb directly from the subject.

κατηγορικός, ή, όν - Affirmative (Arist., *APr.*) Aristotle, *Anterior Analytics* 26a18
> Having the characteristics of agreement with a remark or request.

κατηγορούμενον, τό - Predicate (Ar., *Fr.*) Aristophanes,
Fragments 7.13

>The part of a sentence that contains the verb and conveys
>information about the subject.

κατορθόω - To correct (Ph., *Leg.*) Philo, *On the Sacred Laws of
Allegory* 1.124

>To fix an error or fault.

κεραία, ἡ - Top of a letter (of the alphabet) (A.D., *Synt.*)
Apollonius Dyscolus, *On Syntax* 28.27

>The peak of the letter "A."

κεράννυμι - Crasis, to coalesce by crasis (D.H., *Comp.*)
Dionysius Halicarnassensis, *On Word Order* 22

>In Greek when the word ἐγώ follows the word καί (καὶ
>ἐγώ) they join to become the word κἀγώ.

κεφάλαιον, τό - Chapter (Chor., in *Herm.*) Choricius, in *Hermes*
17.223

>A prominent division in a book.

κεφάλαιος, α, ον - Principal (Ar., *Ra.*) Aristophanes, *Ranae* 854

>Having the characteristic of being first or highest in order
>of rank or importance.

κίνημα, τό - Inflection (Hdn., *Gr.*) Herodianus, *Prosody*
(*Herodiani Technici reliquiae*) 2.265

>The act or process of changing the form of a word in
>order to express a specific grammatical
>concept, idea, function, etc.

κίνησις, ἡ - Inflection (*EM*) *Etymologicum Magnum / Great
Etymological Lexicon* 220.37

>The act or process of changing the form of a word in

order to express a specific grammatical concept, idea, function, etc.

κιονηδόν - Vertical line of a letter (of the alphabet) (D.T., *Ars gram.*) Dionysius Thrax, *Art of Grammar* 183, 191
> Like a line made when writing a capital iota (I).

κίων, ὁ (ἡ) - Column or stone bearing an inscription (Ar., *V.*) Aristophanes, *Vespae Scholia* 105
> Many columns or stones in the ancient world had names or statements engraved on them, especially gravestones.

κλητική, ἡ - Vocative (D.T., *Ars gram.*) Dionysius Thrax, *Art of Grammar* 636.7
> A grammatical category related to verbs that are used to address persons.

κλητικός, ή, όν - Vocative (A.D., *Pron.*) Apollonius Dyscolus, *On Pronouns* 6.9
> A grammatical category related to verbs that are used to address persons.

κλίνω - To inflect (A.D., *Synt.*) Apollonius Dyscolus, *On Syntax* 212.20
> To change the form of a word in order to express a specific grammatical concept, idea, function, etc.

κλίσις, ἡ - Inflection, augment (A.D., *Pron.*; *EM*) Apollonius Dyscolus, *On Pronouns* 12.14; *Etymologicum Magnum / Great Etymological Lexicon* 23.53
> The act of changing the form of a word in order to express a specific grammatical concept, idea, function, etc.

κοιμίζω - To change final acute accent to grave (D.T., *Ars gram.*) Dionysius Thrax, *Art of Grammar* 23 καὶ instead of καί.

κορωνίς, ἡ - Coronis (e.g. breathing mark) (*EM*) *Etymologicum Magnum / Great Etymological Lexicon* 763.10
> The smooth breathing mark found in words such as ἐν.

κουφισμός, ὁ - Elision (Eust.) Eustathius 150.24
> In Greek when ἀλλά is followed by a word that begins with a vowel and becomes ἀλλ᾽ (thus the final alpha is removed).

κρᾶσις, ἡ - Crasis (A.D., *Adv.*) Apollonius Dyscolus, *On Adverbs* 128.2
> When two or more vowels merge. In Greek when the word ἐγώ follows the word καί (καὶ ἐγώ) they join to become the word κἀγώ.

κτητικὴ ἀντωνυμία, ἡ - Possessive pronoun (A.D., *Pron.*) Apollonius Dyscolus, *On Pronouns* 101.18
> A pronoun that expresses ownership or possession of someone or something.

κτητικός, ἡ, όν - Possessive (genitive) (A.D., *Pron.*) Apollonius Dyscolus, *On Pronouns* 16.15
> Expressing ownership or possession of someone or something.

κτλ. (καὶ τὰ λοιπά) - Etcetera (Hyp., *Fr.*) Hyperides, *Fragments* 162.2
> The ancient Greek equivalent of modern English's "etc." (etcetera).

κύριος, α, ον - Proper (noun) (A.D., *Pron.*) Apollonius Dyscolus, *On Pronouns* 10.11
> A name that identifies a noun (e.g. a person, place, etc.).

κῶλον, τό - Clause (Arist., *Rhet.*) Aristotle, *Rhetoric* 1409b13
A grammatical category that consists of a subject and
predicate but which may be indpendent or dependent.

κώλυσις, ἡ - Prohibition (Arist., *Top.*) Aristotle, *Topics* 161a15
A command or law forbidding something.

λέξις, ἡ - Speech, phrase, glossary (Arist., *Rhet.*) Aristotle, *Rhetoric* 1406b1

> A collection or group of words that work together to create a thought, idea, or reference guide.

ληκτικός, ἡ, όν - Terminal (A.D., *Synt.*) Apollonius Dyscolus, *On Syntax* 7.10

> Having the chracteristic of being the final part or portion of a word or sentence.

λῆξις, ἡ - Ending (of word or sentence) (A.D., *Synt.*) Apollonius Dyscolus, *On Syntax* 104.28

> The final part or portion of a word or sentence.

λόγος, ὁ - Word, sentence (A.D., *Synt.*) Apollonius Dyscolus, *On Syntax* 3.6

> An element of speech that contains and conveys meaning.

μάθημα, τό - Lesson, session (Pl., *Smp.*) Plato, *Symposium* 211
A period of time in which teaching occurs or the content
of what is taught.

μακρὰ συλλαβή - Long syllable (D.T., *Ars gram.*) Dionysius
Thrax, *Art of Grammar* 17.4
In English the syllable "ee" in the word "feet" is long. In
the Greek word λόγου the syllable "ου" is long.

μακρός, ά, όν - Long syllable (or vowel) (Ar., *Av.*)
Aristophanes, *Aves* 1131
In English the syllable "ee" in the word "feet" is long. In
the Greek word λόγου the syllable "ου" is long.

μακρότης, ἡ - Length (A.D., *Adv.*) Apollonius Dyscolus, *On
Adverbs* 187.15
The measurement of a syllable, vowel, etc.

μακρύνω - To lengthen (Nic., *Ep.*) Nicolaus I, *Epistles* 30.47
To lengthen the sound of a vowel often through
augmentation, that is, the addition of letters (esp. vowels)
on to the front of a root or stem.

μανθάνω - To learn, understand (Pl., *Euthd.*) Plato, *Euthydemus*
277e
To acquire information, data, knowledge, or skill in
something that has been taught.

μεγεθύνω - To lengthen (A.D., *Adv.*) Apollonius Dyscolus, *On
Adverbs* 193.23

To lengthen the sound of a vowel often through augmentation, that is, the addition of letters (esp. vowels) on to the front of a root or stem.

μείωσις, ἡ - Diminution (Arist., *Cat.*) Aristotle, *Categories* 15a14
>
> The reducing or diminishing someone or something.

μέλαν, τό - Ink (Pl., *Phdr.*) Plato, *Phaedrus* 276c
>
> A liquid (usually dark) used for writing or similar activities.

μέλλων, ὁ - Future (tense) (Pi., *O.*) Pindar, *Olympian Odes* 10.7
>
> A verb tense that anticipates a state or action that will occur (in the future).

μεμβράνα, ἡ - Notebook, tablet, parchment (NT, *2 Ep. Ti.*) *2 Timothy* 4.13
>
> Material used to write words upon.

μερισμός, ὁ - Classification, parsed word (or sentence) (A.D., *Synt.*) Apollonius Dyscolus, *On Syntax* 23.8, 140.11
>
> The arranging of items or parts of items or items or parts that have been arranged.

μέρος, τό - Part (of speech or word) (A.D., *Pron.*) Apollonius Dyscolus, *On Pronouns* 4.6
>
> The grammatical category into which any word might fall.

μεσάζομαι - To insert into the middle (A.D., *Synt.*) Apollonius Dyscolus, *On Syntax* 270.5
>
> To place or put one or more items between other items.

μέση (διάθεσις), ἡ - Middle (voice) (*EM*) *Etymologicum Magnum / Great Etymological Lexicon* 754.18

The action of the verb that is both carried and received by
the subject.

μέση (στιγμή), ἡ - Colon, semicolon (middle point) (Arist.,
Ph.) Aristotle, *Physics* 220a17
> A punctuation mark that indicates a short break or pause
> in a writing. Both the colon and semicolon are denoted by
> the raised dot symbol (·) in Koine.

μέσον, η, ον - Middle (A.D., *Synt.*) Apollonius Dyscolus, *On
Syntax* 276.21
> Referring to the middle voice or, in general, something
> that is in the middle of or between other items.

μεσοσυλλαβία, ἡ - Parenthesis (E., *Med.*) Euripedes, *Medea*
1085
> Either a pair of symbols or markings used to draw
> attention to or include a word or some other part of
> speech, or an insertion into a passage or thought that
> completes the passage or thought.

μεσότης, ἡ - Middle (voice) (A.D., *Synt.*) Apollonius Dyscolus,
On Syntax 211.19
> The action of the verb that is both carried and received by
> the subject.

μεταβατικός, ἡ, όν - Transitive (A.D., *Pron.*) Apollonius
Dyscolus, *On Pronouns* 24.15
> Having the characteristics of being transitive.

μεταγράφω - To copy, transcribe (Luc., *Ind.*) Lucianus, *Against
Indoctum* 4
> To duplicate a thought, comment, idea, etc. To render
> words from one language into another.

μετάθεσις, ἡ - Plagiarism, transposition, metathesis (A.D., *Pron.*; Demetr., *Eloc.*) Apollonius Dyscolus, *On Pronouns* 51.5; Demetrius Phalereus, *On Style* 112

> The act of using someone's work or words as if they were your own. The act of changing letters (whether purposefully or not).

μετάκλισις, ἡ - Changed case (Eust.) Eustathius 15.29

> When the case or case ending of a word is changed.

μεταλαμβάνω - To change dialect, translate (A.D., *Synt.*) Apollonius Dyscolus, *On Syntax* 107.2

> To render words from one language into another.

μεταξύ, τό - Neuter (Arist., *Po.*) Aristotle, *Poetics* 1458a17

> Words often related to "neuter" or "sexless" things; words that, in terms of sexual gender, are arbitrary.

μετασύρω - To change in form (Eust.) Eustathius 32.42

> To add affixes to a root or stem can change the verb's form.

μεταφέρω - To use a metaphor / metaphorically (Arist., *EN.*) Aristotle, *Nichomachean Ethics* 1167a10

> To make one thing represent or symbolize another thing.

μεταφορά, ἡ - Metaphor (Arist., *Po.*) Aristotle, *Poetics* 1457b6

> Something that represents or symbolizes something else.

μεταφορικός, ἡ, όν - Metaphorical (Phld., *Po.*) Philodemus, *On Poems* 2.55

> Having the characteristics of being a metaphor.

μεταφράζω - To paraphrase, translate (Plu., *Cat.Ma.*) Plutarch, *Cato Major* 19

To restate an idea using different words. To render words from one language into another.

μετάφρασις, ἡ - Translation (Plu., *Dem.*) Plutarch, *On Demosthenes* 2.347
> That which is rendered from one language into another.

μετοχή, ἡ - Participle (A.D., *Synt.*) Apollonius Dyscolus, *On Syntax* 15.20
> A word formed from a verb and an adjective that functions as/like an adjective or complement.

μετοχικός, ἡ, όν - Participial (A.D., *Synt.*) Apollonius Dyscolus, *On Syntax* 84.23
> Having the characteristics of being a participle.

μέτρον, τό - Meter (Ar., *Nu.*) Aristophanes, *Clouds* 638
> The rhythm denoted by the structure of a writing.

μετωνυμία, ἡ - Metonymy (one word used for another) (Ps. - Plu., *Vit.Hom.*) Pseudo-Plutarch, *Life of Homer* 23
> The act of using one word to represent another. For example, in English, the use of the word "pig" for "cop."

μικρὰ γράμματα, τά - Lower case letters (Arist., *Pr.*) Aristotle, *Problems* 958a35
> A written form of letters that is smaller than upper case letters. Often called miniscules.

μνήμη, ἡ - Memory, inscription, record (Arist., *Rh.*) Aristotle, *Rhetoric* 1361a34
> Something from the past which has been written down or mentally remembered.

μονόκλιτος, ον - Indeclinable (*EM*) *Etymologicum Magnum / Great Etymological Lexicon* 314.23
> Characteristic of a word that lacks grammatical inflection, that is, it stays the same regardless of case. For example, in Greek the name Μιχαηλ (Michael).

μονοπρόσωπος, ον - Singular (of pronouns) (Hdn., *Gr.*) Herodianus, *Prosody* (*Herodiani Technici reliquiae*) 2.26
> Having the characteristic of being single.

μονοσύλλαβος, ον - Monosyllabic (A.D., *Pron.*) Apollonius Dyscolus, *On Pronouns* 27.2
> Having the characteristic of only having one syllable. For example, the English word "ah."

μονόφθογγος, ἡ - Monophthong (single vowel sound or syllable) (Theodos., *Can.*) Theodosius, *Canons* (*On Grammar*) 68H
> A single vowel or a single vowel sound.

μόριον, τό - Affix (prefix, infix, suffix) (*EM*) *Etymologicum Magnum / Great Etymological Lexicon* 141.47
> A morphological element placed at the front of, in the middle of, or at the end of a word (or word's root or stem).

νόημα, τό - Thought (Pi., *P.*) Pindar, *Pythian Odes* 6.29
   A mental or intellectual result or product of thinking.

νυγμή, ἡ - Punctuation mark (Plu., *Ant.*) Plutarch, *Antonius* 86
   Symbols or markings that denote the organization and
   intentions of a sentence.

O

οἰκειωματικός, ή, όν - Possessive (*EM*) *Etymologicum Magnum / Great Etymological Lexicon* 30.6
>   Characteristic of words that express ownership or possession of someone or something.

ὁμοιόγραφος, ον - Similarly written, a forger (A.D., *Conj.*; Vett.Val.) Apollonius Dyscolus, *On Conjunctions* 258.14; Vettius Valens 74.19
>   Characteristic of a document, perhaps copied, that bears similarities to another document.

ὁμοιόπτωτος, ον - Similar case, similar ending (A.D., *Synt.*) Apollonius Dyscolus, *On Syntax* 124.26
>   Characteristic of words whose case endings are similar. Characteristic of words whose endings are similar, usually in parallel lines of text.

ὁμοιοτέλευτος, ον - Similarly ending, homoeoteleuton (Phld., *Rh.*) Philodemus, *Rhetoric* 1.162
>   Characteristic of words whose endings are similar, usually in parallel lines of text.

ὁμοιόφθογγος, ον - Similarly sounding (*EM*) *Etymologicum Magnum / Great Etymological Lexicon* 169.10
>   Characteristic of two or more words that contain the same sounds.

ὁμοφωνία, ή - Homophone (Arist., *Pol.*) Aristotle, *Politics* 1263b35
>   A word that has the same pronunciation as another word but a different meaning. For example "two" and "to."

ὄνομα, τό - Noun, name, word (A.D., *Synt.*) Apollonius
Dyscolus, *On Syntax* 12.25
> A term that denotes a person, place, thing, or idea.

ὀνομαστικός, ή, όν - Nominative (A.D., *Synt.*) Apollonius
Dyscolus, *On Syntax* 107.4
> A grammatical category usually denoting or pointing to
> the subject of the sentence.

ὀνοματοποιία, ή - Onomatopoeia (Str., *Chr.*) Strabo,
Chrestomathy 14.2.28
> A word formed from the sound associated with it. For
> example the English words "moo" and "meow."

ὀξεῖα, ή - Acute (accent) (A.D., *Pron.*) Apollonius Dyscolus,
On Pronouns 35.10
> The mark or symbol (´) placed over a letter to indicate a
> change in pitch or sound.

ὀξύνω - To pronounce with an acute accent (A.D., *Pron.*)
Apollonius Dyscolus, *On Pronouns* 35.10
> To raise the pitch when pronouncing a word with an
> acute accent.

ὀξύς, εῖα, ύ - Acute (accent) (Pl., *Ti.*) Plato, *Timaeus* 80a
> Characteristic of the mark or symbol (´) placed over a
> letter to indicate a change in pitch or sound.

ὀξύτονος, ον - Acute (accent) (A.D., *Pron.*) Apollonius
Dyscolus, *On Pronouns* 83.15
> Characteristic of the mark or symbol (´) placed over a
> letter to indicate a change in pitch or sound.

ὀργανικόν, τό - Instrumental (Plu., *Cat.Mi.*) Plutarch, *Cato Minor* 4

> A word that functions as a means or agency. In Greek this is often associated with the dative case.

ὀρεκτικός, ή, όν - Conative (Arist., *EN.*) Aristotle, *Nichomachean Ethics* 1102b30

> Characteristic of expressing effort.

ὀρθή, ή - Nominative (A.D., *Pron.*) Apollonius Dyscolus, *On Pronouns* 6.19

> A grammatical category usually denoting or pointing to the subject of the sentence.

ὀρθογραφία, ή - Correct (spelling) (A.D., *Adv.*) Apollonius Dyscolus, *On Adverbs* 165.15

> A word that is written and spelled correctly.

ὀρθοέπεια, ή - Correct pronunciation, speaking (Pl., *Phdr.*) Plato, *Phaedrus* 267c

> The speaking or pronouncing of a word or group of words clearly and correctly.

ὀρθολογέω - To pronounce or speak correctly (Plu., *Mor.*) Plutarch, *Moralia* 2.570e

> To speak or pronounce a word or group of words clearly and correctly.

ὀρθολογία, ή - Correct speech or language (Pl., *Sph.*) Plato, *Sophists* 239b

> A word that is spoken (or written) correctly.

ὀρθός, ή, όν - Direct (speech), correct (spelling) (Pl., *Ti.*) Plato, *Timaeus* 44b

> Speech or discourse that is reports the actual words of the

speaker.

ὁρίζω - To define (Pl., *Chrm.*) Plato, *Charmides* 171a
> To explain the meaning of a thought, concept, word, idea, etc.

ὁριστική, ἡ - Indicative (A.D., *Synt.*) Apollonius Dyscolus, *On Syntax* 31.14
> Related to a verb expressing the reality or realness of a situation.

ὅρος, ὁ - Definition (Chrysipp., *Stoic.*) Chrysippus, *Stoicism* 2.75
> The meaning of a thought, concept, word, idea, etc.

οὐδέτερος, ἡ, όν – Neuter (A.D., *Pron.*) Apollonius Dyscolus, *On Pronouns* 6.19
> Characteristic of words often related to "neuter" or "sexless" things; words that, in terms of sexual gender, are arbitrary.

π

παθητικός, ή, όν - Passive (A.D., *Synt.*) Apollonius Dyscolus, *On Syntax* 150.19
    Having the characteristics of being able to be acted upon.

πάθος, η, ον - Passive (A.D., *Synt.*) Apollonius Dyscolus, *On Syntax* 12.17
    Having the characteristics of being able to be acted upon.

πάπυρος, ὁ (ἡ) - Papyrus (Thephr., *HP.*) Theophrastus, *History of Plants* 4.8.2
    A substance from an Egyptian plant that is used to make a paper-like material for writing on. A document made of papyrus.

παραβολή, ἡ - Parable, comparison (NT, *Ev.Marc.*) *Mark* 12.1
    A story or similarity used to illustrate a point.

παραβολικός, ή, όν - Comparative (of adverbs) (Hom., *Il.*), Homer, *Iliad* 13.2
    Having the characteristic of being comparable.

παραγραφή, ἡ - Division (of sections of a text) (Eust.) Eustathius 107.46
    A portion of a writing that is usually quite prominent.

παράγραφος, ὁ - Paragraph, division that marks a change in speakers (Heph., *Poëm.*) Hephaestio, *On Poems* 5.3
    A prominent division in a chapter.

παραγωγή, ἡ - Origin, derivation (A.D., *Synt.*) Apollonius Dyscolus, *On Syntax* 192.3

The point from which something, such as a word, came into existence.

παράδειγμα, τό - Paradigm, proof from example (Arist., *Rh.*)
Aristotle, *Rhetoric* 1393a27
>The common or usual pattern of how words and/or other grammatical entities form and function.

παραίνεσις, ἡ - Paranesis (paraenesis), exhortation (A., *Eu.*)
Aeschylus, *Eumenides* 707
>A moral instruction or teaching.

παραινετικός, ἡ, όν - Hortatory (AristoStoic.) Aristo Chius, 1.80
>Having the characteristics of a moral instruction or teaching.

παρακείμενος, ὁ - Perfect (tense) (A.D., *Synt.*) Apollonius Dyscolus, *On Syntax* 205.15
>A grammatical category denoting the state or action of a verb that occurred in the past and whose action or state was completed.

παρακέλευσις, ἡ - Exhortation (Phld., *Oec.*) Philodemus, *On Economics* 36J
>A moral instruction or teaching.

παρακελευσματικός, ἡ, όν - Hortatory (Eust.) Eustathius 1393.4
>Having the characteristics of a moral instruction or teaching.

παραλέγω - To cite (Aen. Tact.) Aeneas Tacticus 4.7
>To identify a source of a quotation or proof.

παραλήγουσα, ἡ - Ending, penult (A.D., *Pron.*) Apollonius Dyscolus, *On Pronouns* 11.9

> Either the last or next to last syllable of a word.

παραλήγω - To be penultimate (A.D., *Synt.*) Apollonius Dyscolus, *On Syntax* 255.5

> To be or to be placed on the next to last syllable of a word.

παράλληλος, ον, ότης - Parallel (A.D., *Adv.*) Apollonius Dyscolus, *On Adverbs* 140.13

> Characteristic of either lines of a writing that run side by side or are similar, or one thing that is similar or analogous to another.

παράλογος, ον - Irregular (A.D., *Pron.*) Apollonius Dyscolus, *On Pronouns* 27.26

> Characteristic of a deviation from standard usage or meaning.

παραπληρωματικός, ὁ - Expletive (conjunction or particle) (A.D., *Conj.*) Apollonius Dyscolus, *On Conjunctions* 247.22

> An oath or curse/swear word.

παρασυναπτικός, ὁ - Connective, particle (causal) (A.D., *Conj.*) Apollonius Dyscolus, *On Conjunctions* 220.14

> A word that connects other words, phrases, clauses, sentences, paragraphs, etc.

παρασύνθετος, η, ον - From a compound (A.D., *Synt.*) Apollonius Dyscolus, *On Syntax* 330.5

> A word derived from a compound word, for example, the word "otolaryngology."

παράτασις, ἡ - Imperfect (of tense) (A.D., *Synt.*) Apollonius Dyscolus, *On Syntax* 70.27

> Denoting the state or action of a verb that occurred in the past and whose action or state was either incomplete or durative.

παρατατικός, ὁ - Imperfect (tense) (A.D., *Synt.*) Apollonius Dyscolus, *On Syntax* 10.19

> Denoting the state or action of a verb that occurred in the past and whose action or state was either incomplete or durative.

παρατελευταῖος, α, ον - Penultimate (Ath.) Athenaeus 3.106c

> Characteristic of being placed on the next to last syllable of a word.

παρατέλευτος, ον - Penultimate (Ar., *Pl.*) Aristophanes, *Plutus* 598

> To be or to be placed on the next to last syllable of a word.

παρεγγράφω - To write next to, interpolate (Aeschin., *Ep.*) Aeschines, *Epistles* 3.74

> To insert a word or group of words inserted into a sentence, text, story, etc. (after its completion).

παρεμβάλη, ἡ - Interpolation (Alex.Aphr., in Top.) Alexander Aphrodisiensis, in *Topics* (by Aristotle) 309.27

> A word or group of words inserted into a sentence, text, story, etc. (after its completion).

παρεμφατικός, ἡ, όν - Indicative, finite (A.D., *Pron.*; D.H., *Comp.*) Apollonius Dyscolus, *On Pronouns*; Dionysius Halicarnassensis, *On Word Order* 5

> Related to a verb expressing the reality or realness of a

situation.

παρένθεσις, ἡ - Parenthesis, interjection (Hermog., *Id.*)
Hermogenes, *On Ideas* 1.12
>Either a pair of symbols or markings used to draw
>attention to or include a word or some other part of
>speech, or an insertion into a passage or thought that
>completes the passage or thought.

παρένθετος, ον - Interpolated (Eust.) Eustathius 67.29
>Characteristic of a word or group of words inserted into a
>sentence, text, story, etc. (after its completion).

παρεντίθημι - To interpolate (Hermog., *Id.*) Hermogenes, *On
Ideas* 2.10
>To insert a word or group of words inserted into a
>sentence, text, story, etc. (after its completion).

παρηχητικός, ἡ, όν - Alliterative (Eust.) Eustathius 452.4
>Having the characteristics of alliteration.

παροιχόμενος, η, ον - Past (of the) (A.D., *Adv.*) Apollonius
Dyscolus, *On Adverbs* 123.17
>Related to a verb expressing that something occurred in
>the past or in past time.

παρών, οὖσα, όν - Present (tense) (Pl., *Tht.*) Plato, *Theaetetus*
186b
>Related to a verb expressing the reality or realness of a
>situation.

πατρικός, ἡ, όν - Genitive (Choerob., in Theod.) Choerboscus,
cited in Theodorus 1.111 H (see *Anthologia Graeca*)
>A characteristic that usually indicates possession but can
>also indicate source, measure, etc.

πεζός, ἡ, όν - Prosaic (of prose) (D.H., *Comp.*) Dionysius
Halicarnassensis, *On Word Order* 6
> Having the characteristics of being prose.

πεντάπτωτος, ον - Having five cases (Priscian., *Inst.*)
Priscianus, *Institutes* 5.76
> Characteristic of a verb that is said to have the
> nominative, genitive, dative, accusative, and vocative
> cases.

περιγράφω - To place in brackets (Demonic.) Demonicus 1.3
> To place a word or statement in brackets.

περίκλασις, ἡ - Circumflex (accent) (D.T., *Ars gram.*)
Dionysius Thrax, *Art of Grammar* 630.2
> The (˜) mark or symbol placed over a letter to indicate a
> change in pitch or sound.

περίοδος, ἡ - Period (final mark/point) (Heph., *Poëm.*)
Hephaestio, *On Poems* 3.5
> A temporary stop or a repetitive rhythm often marked
> with the symbol (.).

περισπωμένη, ἡ - Circumflex (accent) (A.D., *Pron.*) Apollonius
Dyscolus, *On Pronouns* 93.17
> The (˜) mark or symbol placed over a letter to indicate a
> change in pitch or sound.

περισπώμενος, η, ον - Pronounce with a circumflex (A.D.,
Pron.) Apollonius Dyscolus, *On Pronouns* 33.24
> To raise the pitch of a word and then to immediately drop
> the pitch of a word.

περίστασις, ἡ - Contraction (Vett.Val.) Vettius Valens 14.2

When a word form takes an affix or suffix without and as a result changes or morphs.

περιστίζω - To punctuate (*EM*) *Etymologicum Magnum* / *Great Etymological Lexicon* 169.37
> To use symbols or markings in a writing to denote the organization and intentions of a sentence.

πεῦσις, ἡ - Question (D.H., *Dem.*) Dionysius Halicarnassensis, *On Demosthenes* 54
> An expression used to ask for data or information about someone or something.

πευστικός, ἡ, όν - Interrogatory, interrogative (A.D., *Adv.*) Apollonius Dyscolus, *On Adverbs* 193.26
> Having the characteristics of being a question.

πίναξ[ι], ὁ - Table of contents, glossary (Plu., *Sull.*) Plutarch, *Sulla* 26
> A list of titles, chapters, or significant words located at either the front or back of a writing such as a book.

πινακίδιον, τό - Tablet (wooden) (Plu., *Eum.*) Plutarch, *Eumenedes* 1
> Materials used for writing on. In antiquity tablets were made of various materials including wax, wood, stone, etc.

πλάγιος, α, ον - Oblique (case) (A.D., *Pron.*) Apollonius Dyscolus, *On Pronouns* 23.1
> The genitive, dative, or accusative case. Any of the cases but the nominative and vocative cases.

πλεονάζω - To use a pleonasm (extra words), to be redundant (*EM*) *Etymologicum Magnum / Great Etymological Lexicon* 84.18

> To use more words than are needed to make a point or convey meaning.

πλεονασμός, ὁ - Pleonasm (A.D., *Synt.*) Apollonius Dyscolus, *On Syntax* 267.14

> The act of using more words than are needed to make a point or convey meaning.

πληθυντικός, ή, όν - Plural (A.D., *Pron.*) Apollonius Dyscolus, *On Pronouns* 11.2

> Having the characteristic of not being single; having more than one.

πληθυσμός, ὁ - Pluralization (Dam., *Pr.*) Damascius, *On Principles* 53

> The act of making something plural.

πληρόω - To complete (a document) (Lyd., *Mag.*) Lydus, *On Roman Magistrates* 3.11

> To complete a writing such as a book.

πνεῦμα, τό - Aspirate (A.D., *Adv.*) Apollonius Dyscolus, *On Adverbs* 147.18

> A word where the "h" sound is pronounced before a vowel or vowel pair (diphthong).

πνευματικός, ή, όν - Having to do with breathing(s) (Arist., *GA.*) Aristotle, *Animal Species* 781a31

> For instance, the rough or smooth breathing marks (’ or ‘).

ποίημα, τό - Poem (Pl., *Phd.*) Plato, *Phaedo* 60d

A writing or speech that is often rhythmical,
metaphorical, song-like, and contains rhyming words.

πολύλεξις, ι - Wordy (having many words) (D.T., *Ars gram.*)
Dionysius Thrax, *Art of Grammar* 25H
Characteristic of using big words or too many words.

πολυσύλλαβος, ον - Polysyllabic (D.H., *Comp.*) Dionysius
Halicarnassensis, *On Word Order* 11
Characteristic of having multiple syllables.

ποσός, ή, όν - Quantity (Arist., *EN.*) Aristotle, *Nichomachean
Ethics* 1158b31
The amount or number of persons or things.

πρᾶγμα, τό - Action, affair, deed, circumstance (X., *HG.*)
Xenophon, *Greek History* 7.1.17
An event that has or is or will take place.

πραγματεία, ή - Treatise (Arist., *Top.*) Aristotle, *Topics* 100a18
A composition that focuses on a specific subject.

προαίρεσις, ή - Purpose (Arist., *EN.*) Aristotle, *Nichomachean
Ethics* 1094a2
The reason something is created, used, or done.

πρόθεσις, ή - Preposition (A.D., *Synt.*) Apollonius Dyscolus,
On Syntax 305.24
A word that denotes a relationship between a noun or
pronoun and other words in a sentence, clause, or phrase.

προθετικός, ή, όν - Prepositional (A.D., *Synt.*) Apollonius
Dyscolus, *On Syntax* 305.24
Having the characteristics of being a preposition or being
governed by a preposition.

προληπτικός, ή, όν - Proleptic (A.D., *Pron.*) Apollonius
Dyscolus, *On Pronouns* 10.22
> Having the characteristics of being proleptic (see
> πρόληψις, ἡ).

πρόληψις, ἡ - Proplepsis (Hermog., *Meth.*) Hermogenes, *On
The Method of Effective Speech* 10
> Something spoken of (often anachronistically) before it
> happens (e.g. like a flash-forward).

προπαραλήγουσα, ἡ - Ending (of a word) (A.D., *Pron.*)
Apollonius Dyscolus, *On Pronouns* 11.9
> A case ending or suffix.

προπαροξυντικός, ή, όν - Proparoxytonic (acute accent on the
antepenult) (Eust.) Eustathius 75.37
> Having the characteristic of being or being on the
> antepenult.

προπαροξύνω - To make proparoxytonic (A.D., *Pron.*)
Apollonius Dyscolus, *On Pronouns* 30.7
> To place an accent on the antepenult.

προπαροξύτονος, ον - Proparoxytonic (acute accent on the
antepenult) (D.T., *Ars gram.*) Dionysius Thrax, *Art of Grammar*
108 U
> Having the characteristic of being or being on the
> antepenult.

προσαγορευτικός, ή, όν - Vocative (case) (*Stoic.*) *Stoicorum
Veterum Fragmenta / Old Stoic Fragments* 2.61
> Characteristic of nouns that are used to address persons.

προσηγορία, ἡ - Appellation, common noun - (D.T., *Ars gram.*)
Dionysius Thrax, *Art of Grammar* 634.6

Either the act of giving a name or title, or the name or title
itself.

προσθήκη, ἡ - Particle, epithet (Demetr., *Eloc.*) Demetrius
Phalereus, *On Style* 55

A particle is a word that does not inflect and which is
usually very short. In English "not" is often considered a
particle.

πρόσπνευσις, ἡ - Aspiration (Phld., *Po.*) Philodemus, *On
Poems* 2.5

Often understood as the act of pronouncing the "h" sound
particularly before a vowel or vowel pair (diphthong).

προσπνέω - To pronounce with rough breathing (A.D., *Pron.*)
Apollonius Dyscolus, *On Pronouns* 55.23

To pronounce the "h" sound particularly before a vowel
or vowel pair (diphthong).

προσῳδία, ἡ - Accent (mark), pitch (Pl., *R.*) Plato, *Republic*
399a

A symbol or mark that denotes inflection, pitch, or accent
change in a word.

προσωποποιία, ἡ - Personification, change of grammatical
person (A.D., *Adv.*) Apollonius Dyscolus, *On Adverbs* 131.16

The application of human characteristics to something
that is not human.

προτακτικός, ἡ, όν – Prepositive (A.D., *Synt.*) Apollonius
Dyscolus, *On Syntax* 306.15

Having the characteristics of a word, letter, or group of
words or letters placed before other words, letters, or

groups of words or letters.

προταξις, ἡ - Prefix, prepositive (A.D., *Adv.*) Apollonius
Dyscolus, *On Adverbs* 125.7
A word, letter, or group of words or letters placed before
other words, letters, or groups of words or letters.

προτασις, ἡ - Protasis (D.L.) Diogenes Laertius 3.52
The "if" part of an "if/then" statement.

προτάσσω - To prefix, make prepositive (A.D., *Pron.*)
Apollonius Dyscolus, *On Pronouns* 116.6
To place a letter or word before another letter or word.

πρότερος, η, ον - Previous, prior, first (Arist., *Pol.*) Aristotle,
Politics 1316a16
Something that came first in order, time, or significance.

προφορά, ἡ - Pronunciation (D.H., *Dem.*) Dionysius
Halicarnassensis, *On Demosthenes* 22
An enunciated or spoken sound.

πρῶτα μέρη, τά - Principal parts (D.H., *Comp.*) Dionysius
Halicarnassensis, *On Word Order* 74-75
The forms of a verb from which its inflected forms can be
realized.

πρωτότυπος, ον - Primary, prototypical (Dam., *Pr.*) Damascius,
On Principles 340
Characteristic of a first or original example or type which
subsequent types are based on.

πτῶσις, ἡ - Case (Arist., *SE.*) Aristotle, *Sophistic Refutations*
173b27
A grammatical system, usually denoted by inflection, that

relates substantives to the other words in a sentence.

πτωτικός, ή, όν - Inflectable (A.D., *Pron.*) Apollonius
Dyscolus, *On Pronouns* 9.5
> Having the characteristic of being able to undergo
> inflection.

πυσματικός, ή, όν - Interrogatory (A.D., *Pron.*) Apollonius
Dyscolus, *On Pronouns* 27.16
> Having the characteristics of being a question.

ῥῆμα, τό - Verb, sentence, predicate (Pl., *Sph.*, Cra.; Arist., Int.)
Plato, *Sophists* 262a, Cratylus 399b; Aristotle, *On Interpretation*
16b6
> A grammatical category whose words denote an action or
> state of being. The part of a sentence containing the verb.

ῥηματικός, ή, όν - Verbal (A.D., *Adv.*) Apollonius Dyscolus,
On Adverbs 135.14
> Having the characteristics of being related to a verb.

ῥίζα, ή - Root (Pl., *Ti.*) Plato, *Timaeus* 81c
> The part of a word that does not change and to which
> affixes are added.

σ

σαφής, ές - Prominent, vivid (Pl., *Prt.*) Plato, *Protagoras* 352a
Having the characteristic of being important or
distinguished.

σέλις, ἡ - Page, column of writing (Hsch.; LXX, *Je.*) Hesychius
383.1; *Jeremiah* 43 (36).23
A portion of a writing or the material upon which a text is
written.

σελίς, ἡ (σελίδες) - Column (in a writing), white space between
columns (Phan., *AP.*; Suid.) Phanias, 6.295 (see *Anthologia
Graeca*); Suidas (N/A)
A vertical portion of a composition.

σημαντικός, ή, όν - Significant (semantic) (Arist., *Int.*)
Aristotle, *On Interpretation* 16a19
Having the characteristic of carrying great importance.

σημεῖον, τό - Mark, note, sign (Heph., *Poëm.*) Hephaestio, *On
Poems* 73c
A word or symbol used to draw attention to particular
thoughts, ideas, or words.

σολοικίζω - To use a solecism (make a grammatical error)
(A.D., *Synt.*) Apollonius Dyscolus, *On Syntax* 199.14
To use an incorrect word or to use a word incorrectly.

σολοικισμός, ὁ - Solecism (grammatical error) (A.D., *Synt.*)
Apollonius Dyscolus, *On Syntax* 198.8
A word used incorrectly, for example, a slang term in
speech or writing.

στιγμή, ἡ - Punctuation mark, period, colon (D.T., *Ars gram.*)
Dionysius Thrax, *Art of Grammar* 630.6
> Symbols or markings that denote the organization and intentions of a sentence. A temporary stop or a repetitive rhythm often marked with the symbol (.).

στίζω - To punctuate (Herm., in *Phdr.*) Hermias Alexandrinus in *Phaedrus* 84a
> To use symbols or markings in a writing to denote the organization and intentions of a sentence.

στίχος, ὁ - Verse, line (of a writing), chapter (Heph., *Poëm.*)
Hephaestio, *On Poems* 1
> Typically a small portion of a writing.

στοιχεῖον, τό - Elements, sounds (A.D., *Synt.*) Apollonius Dyscolus, *On Syntax* 313.7
> The basic building blocks of a word.

στοιχείωσις, ἡ - Elementary/basic teaching (Phld., *Rh.*)
Philodemus, *Rhetoric* 1.104
> The principles or rules of grammar and speech taught at an early age.

στοιχειωτής, ὁ - Early grammar teacher (A.D., *Synt.*)
Apollonius Dyscolus, *On Syntax* 309.5
> Someone who teaches the basic principles or rules of grammar and speech to beginning learners.

συγγραφεύς, ὁ - Prose author (Pl, *Phdr.*) Plato, *Phaedrus* 235c
> Someone who composes prose literature.

συγγραφόμενον, τό - Subscript (iota) (D.T., *Ars gram.*)
Dionysius Thrax, *Art of Grammar* 30

A letter or character written below another letter. In Greek the letter iota (ι) is often subscripted.

συγκλίνω - To decline (A.D., *Synt.*) Apollonius Dyscolus, *On Syntax* 102.11
> To analyze a word in order to figure out its declension.

συγκοπή, ἡ - Syncope (loss of one or more letters in a word) (A.D., *Adv.*) Apollonius Dyscolus, *On Adverbs* 169.15
> The omission of letters or sounds in a word or phrase. For example, in English, "'Sup?" for "What's up?"

συγκρίνω - To compare, combine (Arist., *Rh.*) Aristotle, *Rhetoric* 1368a21
> To show similar traits between two items. The act of joining two items.

σύγκρισις, ἡ - Comparison (Arist., *Top.*) Aristotle, *Topics* 102b15
> The act of showing similar traits between two items.

συγκριτικός, ἡ, όν - Comparative degree (A.D., *Synt.*) Apollonius Dyscolus, *On Syntax* 58.28
> The comparative form of an adjective; a diminutive or superlative.

συζυγία, ἡ - Conjugation (A.D., *Adv.*) Apollonius Dyscolus, *On Adverbs* 198.6
> The different forms of a word in light of grammatical categories such as tense, voice, mood, person, and number. A word that has been conjugated.

σύζυγος, ον - Conjugated, joined (A.D., *Pron.*) Apollonius Dyscolus, *On Pronouns* 51.9
> Having the characteristic of being inflected with regard

to items such as tense, voice, mood, etc.

συλλαβή, ἡ - Syllable (Luc., *Jud. Voc.*) Lucianus, *The Consonants at Law* 2.6

> A group of letters having one vowel sound.

συμβολικός, ἡ, όν - Symbolic (Iamb., *VP.*) Iamblichus, *Life of Pythagorus* 5.20

> Having the characteristics of being a symbol or being related to a symbol.

συμβουλευτικός, ἡ, όν – Deliberative (Arist., *Rh.*) Aristotle, *Rhetoric* 1358b7

> Characteristic of speech having to do with politics or persuasion.

συμπλεκτικός, ἡ, όν - Copulative (conjunction) (A.D., *Adv.*) Apollonius Dyscolus, *On Adverbs* 218.14

> A word that connects a subject and the predicate in a sentence.

σύμφωνον, τό - Consonant (A.D., *Pron.*) Apollonius Dyscolus, *On Pronouns* 11.2

> Any letter that is not a vowel. In English, for example, "d," "g," "p," etc.

σύναρθρος, ἡ - Possessive pronoun, with the article (A.D., *Pron.*) Apollonius Dyscolus, *On Pronouns* 95.16

> A pronoun that expresses ownership or possession of someone or something.

συναγωγή, ἡ - Collection (of laws, writings, etc.) (Arist., *EN.*) Aristotle, *Nichomachean Ethics* 1181b7

> A group of words or texts.

συναίρεσις, ἡ - Synaeresis, contraction (A.D., *Adv.*) Apollonius Dyscolus, *On Adverbs* 132.25
>The process of two adjacent vowels joining to become a diphthong.

συναλιφή, ἡ - Crasis, synaeresis, running together of sounds or words (A.D., *Synt.*) Apollonius Dyscolus, *On Syntax* 140.14
>In Greek when the word ἐγώ follows the word καί (καὶ ἐγώ) they join to become the word κἀγώ.

συναλοιφή, ἡ - Crasis, synaeresis, running together of sounds or words (A.D., *Synt.*) Apollonius Dyscolus, *On Syntax* 140.14
>In Greek when the word ἐγώ follows the word καί (καὶ ἐγώ) they join to become the word κἀγώ.

συναπτικός, ἡ, όν - Conditional / hypothetical conjunction (A.D., *Conj.*) Apollonius Dyscolus, *On Conjunctions* 218.11
>Having the characteristics of requiring a condition to be met.

σύναρθρος, ον - Articular (A.D., *Pron.*) Apollonius Dyscolus, *On Pronouns* 13.6
>Having the characteristics of being related to the article.

συνάρτησις, ἡ - Construction (grammatical), combination (A.D., *Synt.*) Apollonius Dyscolus, *On Syntax* 17.8
>A construction or pattern related to grammar.

συνδεσμικός, ἡ, όν - Conjunctive (A.D., *Conj.*) Apollonius Dyscolus, *On Conjunctions* 235.5
>Having the characteristics of or being related to a conjunction.

σύνδεσμος, ὁ - Conjunction (Arist., *Rh.*) Aristotle, *Rhetoric* 1407a20

A grammatical category whose words make connections
between words, phrases, clauses, sentences, paragraphs,
etc.

συνδετικός, ή, όν - Conjunctive, connective (A.D., *Synt.*)
Apollonius Dyscolus, *On Syntax* 18.13
> A word that connects other words, phrases, clauses,
> sentences, paragraphs, etc.

σύνθετος, η, ον - Compound, complex (Aristo., *Po.*) Aristotle,
Poetics 1456b35
> Parts of a word or sentence joined to form a whole.

συνίζησις, ή - Metaplasm (sound change, synizesis) (*EM*)
Etymologicum Magnum / Great Etymological Lexicon 279.8
> The act of a word's spelling and sound undergoing
> change.

σύνοδος, ή - Agreement (A.D., *Synt.*) Apollonius Dyscolus, *On
Syntax* 28.11
> The subject and verb agree in person, number, and
> gender.

συνοπτικός, ή, όν - Synoptic (Pl., *R.*) Plato, *Republic* 537c
> Having the characteristics of being able to undergo a
> synopsis.

σύνοψις, ή - Synopsis (D.H., *Th.*) Dionysius Halicarnassensis,
On Thucydides 6
> A side by side comparison of two or more items such as
> writings.

σύνταγμα, τό - Syntactic element (A.D., *Adv.*) Apollonius
Dyscolus, *On Adverbs* 122.17
> A part or portion of a sentence.

σύνταξις, ἡ - Syntax (A.D., *Conj.*) Apollonius Dyscolus, *On Conjunctions* 214.7

> The arrangement of words and phrases to form sentences.

συντελής, ἡ (ὁ) - Perfect, complete (A.D., *Synt.*) Apollonius Dyscolus, *On Syntax* 252.9

> Denoting the state or action of a verb that occurred in the past and whose action or state was completed.

συντελικός, ἡ, όν - Aoristic, completed (A.D., *Synt.*) Apollonius Dyscolus, *On Syntax* 70.9

> Having the characteristics of being related to the aorist tense.

συντελικός, τό - Aorist (Phryn., *PS.*) Phrynicus, *Sophistic Preparations* 315

> A verb form that denotes the past tense without suggesting whether what took place in the past was habitual or has ongoing effects.

συνώνυμον, τό - Synonym (A.D., *Synt.*) Apollonius Dyscolus, *On Syntax* 199.27

> A word that means the same thing as another word.

συριγμός, ὁ - Hissing sound (of a letter such as a sibilant) (D.H., *Comp.*) Dionysius Halicarnassensis, *On Word Order* 14

> Usually heard in words containing s, x, or z. In Greek σ, ζ, or ξ.

συσσημαίνω - To acquire meaning through context (A.D., *Synt.*) Apollonius Dyscolus, *On Syntax* 9.16

> To figure out what a word means based on the context in which it is used.

σφάλμα, τό - Mistake, error (Pl., *Tht.*) Plato, *Theaetetus* 168a
 An incorrect portion of something spelled, written, or spoken.

σχῆμα, τό - Grammatical form (A.D., *Pron.*) Apollonius Dyscolus, *On Pronouns* 17.25
 A particular aspect, detail, or pattern related to grammar.

τ

τὰ μέρη τοῦ λόγου - Parts of speech (A.D., *Pron.*) Apollonius Dyscolus, *On Pronouns* 18.5

> The categories to which words belong based on their syntactical functions.

τὰ στοιχεῖα τῆς λέξεως - Parts of speech (D.H., *Rh.*) Dionysius Halicarnassensis, *On Rhetoric* 7.2

> The categories to which words belong based on their syntactical functions.

τελευτή, ἡ - Ending (of word or sentence) (Arist., *Rh.*) Aristotle, *Rhetoric* 1420b2

> That which is heard or seen at the end of a word or sentence; a case ending.

τελικός, ἡ, όν - Final (letter or word) (D.T., *Ars gram.*) Dionysius Thrax, *Art of Grammar* 632.9

> Characteristic of that which is heard or seen at the end of a word or sentence; a case ending.

τέλος, τό - End (of a word or sentence) (A.D., *Pron.*) Apollonius Dyscolus, *On Pronouns* 12.25

> That which is heard or seen at the end of a word or sentence; a case ending.

τέχνη, ἡ - Art, skill, method, system (Arist., *Rh.*) Aristotle, *Rhetoric* 1354a11

> The art or system of grammar or rhetoric or logic.

τεχνογραφέω - To write grammar rules (Phld., *Rh.*) Philodemus, *Rhetoric* 1.170

For example, in a grammar textbook.

τίτλος, ὁ - Title (Just., *Nov.*) Justinianus, *Novels* 29.4
The name given to a composition.

τόνος, ὁ - Accent (mark), pitch (A.D., *Pron.*) Apollonius
Dyscolus, *On Pronouns* 8.8
A symbol or mark that denotes inflection, pitch, or accent
change in a word.

τονόω - To accentuate (place an accent upon) (PS. -Zonar., *Lex.*)
Pseudo-Zonaras, *Lexicon* "ταυ" 1739.3
To place an accent on the antepenult, penult, or ultima.

τριγένεια, ἡ - Substantive with all three genders (A.D., *Synt.*)
Apollonius Dyscolus, *On Syntax* 212.23
And adjective that can be used across all three genders.

τρίφθογγος, ἡ - Triphthong (Tz., *H.*) Joannes Tzetzes, The
Chiliades (Or: *Book of Histories*) 12.242
A joining of three vowels that become pronounced as one
syllable.

τύπος, ὁ - Form, type, pattern, text, rough draft (A.D., *Synt.*;
Anon. in Phot., *Bibl.*) Apollonius Dyscolus, *On Syntax* 278.25;
Anonymous in Photius, *Bibliography* 491b
A particular aspect, detail, or pattern related to a speech or
composition.

υγρός, ά, όν - Liquified or nasalic (D.T., *Ars gram.*) Dionysius Thrax, *Art of Grammar* 632.9

Having the characteristics of or being related to a liquid or nasal.

ύπακούω - To understand a concept (even when a word is omitted) (A.D., *Synt.*) Apollonius Dyscolus, *On Syntax* 22.21

To comprehend the meaning of an idea.

ύπαλλαγή, ή - Hypallage (reversal of two syntactically related words) (A.D., *Synt.*) Apollonius Dyscolus, *On Syntax* 209.6

An inversion of word order for dramatic effect as with hyperbaton. This is often found in Dr. Seuss books.

ύπαρκτικός, ή, όν - Substantive (A.D., *Synt.*) Apollonius Dyscolus, *On Syntax* 65.13

Having the characteristics of a noun or adjective.

ύπερβατός, ή, όν - Hyperbatonic (transposed words or clauses) (Arist., *Rh.Al.*) Aristotle, *Rhetoric to Alexander* 1438a28

An interruption of normal word order for dramatic effect. This is very prominent in poetry.

ύπερθετικός, ή, όν - Superlative degree (A.D., *Adv.*) Apollonius Dyscolus, *On Adverbs* 167.26

A type or form of an adjective that suggests the greatest or least of something.

ύπερσυντελικός, ό - Pluperfect (tense) (A.D., *Synt.*) Apollonius Dyscolus, *On Syntax* 281.6

Denoting the state or action of a verb that started in the

past, was repeated for a while, and whose action or state finally came to completion.

ὑπόθεσις, ἡ - Subject (of a writing) (D.H., *Pomp.*) Dionysius Halicarnassensis, *Letter to Pompey* 3
>A person, place, or thing being discussed in a writing.

ὑποθετικός, ἡ, όν - Conditional, hypothetical (Arr., *Epict.*) Arrianus, *Writings on Epictetus* 1.7.22
>Having the characteristics of requiring a condition to be met.

ὑποκείμενον, τό - Subject (A.D., *Synt.*) Apollonius Dyscolus, *On Syntax* 122.17
>A person, place, or thing denoting a state or action in a sentence.

ὑποκοριστικός, ἡ, όν - Diminutive (D.T., *Ars gram.*) Dionysius Thrax, *Art of Grammar* 634.25
>Characteristic of a word or affix that denotes smallness.

ὑπολαμβάνω - To understand (Pl., *Prt.*) Plato, *Protagoras* 341b
>To comprehend the meaning of an idea.

ὑποστιγμή, ἡ - Colon, comma (D.T., *Ars gram.*) Dionysius Thrax, *Art of Grammar* 630.14
>A mark or action signifying a brief suspension of speech or writing.

ὑποτακτικός, ἡ, όν - Subjunctive (D.T., *Ars gram.*) Dionysius Thrax, *Art of Grammar* 638.8
>Having the characteristic of the verbal mood in which is wished for, hoped for, or imagined.

ὑποτακτιὸν ἄρθρον, τό - Relative pronoun (Eust.) Eustathius 387.15
> A pronoun that can function as a subject, object, or possessive pronoun (e.g. who, that, whose).

ὑπόταξις, ἡ - Postposition, subordination (A.D., *Pron.*) Apollonius Dyscolus, *On Pronouns* 116.5
> A word or clause that is postpositive or subordinate.

ὑποτάσσω - To govern the subjunctive (*EM*) *Etymologicum Magnum / Great Etymological Lexicon* 471.16
> To bring into conformity with the usage of the subjunctive mood.

ὕπτιος, α, ον - Passive (D.L.) Diogenes Laertius 7.43, 7.64
> Having the characteristics of being able to be acted upon.

ὕστερος, α, ον - Subsequent (D.L.) Diogenes Laertius 7.10
> Having the characteristic of being after something.

φθόγγος, ὁ - Sound (Ar., *Av.*) Aristophanes, *Aves* 1198
Audible noises heard with the ear.

φράσις, ἡ - Phrase (Ar., *Nu.*) Aristophanes, *Clouds* 488
A small collection or group of words that work together to create a thought or idea.

φύσις, ἡ - Gender (Ar., *Lys.*) Aristophanes, *Lysistrata Scholia* 92
Linguistic category that identifies whether a word is masculine, feminine, or neuter.

φωνή, ἡ - Sound (Pl., *Tht.*) Plato, *Theaetetus* 203b
Audible noises heard with the ear.

φωνῆεν, τό - Vowel (S., *Aj.*) Sophocles, *Ajax* 16
A letter of the alphabet that is not a consonant. In English the main vowels are: a, e, i, o, u.

φωνητικός, ή, όν - Phonetic, vocal(ized) (Porph., *Abst.*) Porphyrius Tyrius, *On Abstinence*, 3.3
Having the characteristic of being related to sound.

χ

χαρακτήρ, ὁ - Style, form, letter, character (Hp., *Epid.*)
Hippocrates, *Epidemics* 3.1
> The letters "b" or "c" or any other such character.

χαρακτηριστικός, ή, όν - Characteristic (of) (A.D., *Synt.*)
Apollonius Dyscolus, *On Syntax* 103.17
> A trait belonging to a person or thing.

χάρτης, ὁ - Paper (papyrus - sheet/piece of) (LXX, *Is.*) *Isaiah* 8.1
> Material used to write words upon.

χιασμός, ὁ - Chiasm (Hermog., *Inv.*) Hermogenes, *On the Invention of Arguments* 4.3
> A device that forms an AB / BA pattern thus giving a nice parallel or symmetrical effect.

χρέια, ή - Maxim, anecdote (Hermog., *Prog.*) Hermogenes, *Progymnasmata* 3
> A trustworthy saying or proposition.

χρῆμα, τό - Thing, item, matter, affair (Hes., *Op.*) Hesiod, *Works and Days* 344, 402
> An object or event.

χρονικός, ή, όν - Temporal (A.D., *Pron.*) Apollonius Dyscolus, *On Pronouns* 15.24
> Having the characteristic of dealing with time.

χρόνος, ὁ - Tense, time (A.D., *Adv.*) Apollonius Dyscolus, *On Adverbs* 123.17

    Referring to an event or situation in time.

ψιλόν, τό - Smooth (breathing) (A.D., *Adv.*) Apollonius
Dyscolus, *On Adverbs* 148.9
> The breathing mark found in words such as ἐν.

ψιλός, ή, όν - Smooth (breathing) (A.D., *Adv.*) Apollonius
Dyscolus, *On Adverbs* 148.9
> Characteristic of the smooth breathing mark which is
> found in words such as ἐν.

Part 2

ENGLISH – GREEK

A

Accent (mark), pitch - προσῳδία, ἡ (Pl., *R.*) Plato, *Republic* 399a
> A symbol or mark that denotes inflection, pitch, or accent change in a word.

Accent (mark), pitch - τόνος, ὁ (A.D., *Pron.*) Apollonius Dyscolus, *On Pronouns* 8.8
> A symbol or mark that denotes inflection, pitch, or accent change in a word.

Accusative - αἰτιατική, ἡ (D.T., *Ars gram.*) Dionysius Thrax, *Art of Grammar*, 636.6; (A.D., *Pron.*) Apollonius Dyscolus, *On Pronouns* 11.9
> A grammatical case that denotes the "object" of either a transitive verb or a preposition.

Accusative - αἰτιατικός, ή, όν (D.T., *Ars gram.*) Dionysius Thrax, *Art of Grammar* 636.6; (A.D., Pron.) Apollonius Dyscolus, *On Pronouns* 11.9
> Having the characteristic of being a grammatical case that denotes the "object" of either a transitive verb or a preposition.

Action, affair, deed, circumstance - πρᾶγμα, τό (X., *HG.*) Xenophon, *Greek History* 7.1.17
> An event that has or is or will take place.

Active - δραστήριος, ον (D.H., *Th.*) Dionysius Halicarnassensis, *On Thucydides* 24
> Characteristic of the state of being or action related to the subject.

Active - δραστικός, ή, όν (*Stoic.*) *Stoicorum Veterum Fragmenta / Old Stoic Fragments* 2.133, 2.134
> Characteristic of the state of being or action related to the subject.

Active - ἐνεργητικός, ή, όν (A.D., *Adv.*) Apollonius Dyscolus, *On Adverbs* 161.18
> Characteristic of the state of being or action related to the subject.

Acute (accent) - ὀξεῖα, ή (A.D., *Pron.*) Apollonius Dyscolus, *On Pronouns* 35.10
> The mark or symbol (´) placed over a letter to indicate a change in pitch or sound.

Acute (accent) - ὀξύτονος, ον (A.D., *Pron.*) Apollonius Dyscolus, *On Pronouns* 83.15
> Characteristic of the mark or symbol (´) placed over a letter to indicate a change in pitch or sound.

Acute (accent) -ὀξύς, εῖα, ύ (Pl., *Ti.*) Plato, *Timaeus* 80a
> Characteristic of the mark or symbol (´) placed over a letter to indicate a change in pitch or sound.

Address - ἐπιφώνησις, ή (Phld., *Lib.*) Philodemus, *On Bold Speech* 14O
> An act or form of speaking to another person.

Adjectival - ἐπίθετος, ον (D.T., *Ars gram.*) Dionysius Thrax, *Art of Grammar* 636.9
> Having the characteristics of being an adjective.

Adjective - ἐπίθετον, τό (ἐπιθετικόν) (A.D., *Synt.*) Apollonius Dyscolus, *On Syntax* 41.15

A grammatical category consisting of words that modify nouns.

Adverb - ἐπίρρημα, τό (D.H., *Comp.*) Dionysius Halicarnassensis, *On Word Order* 2
> A modifier that qualifies verbs, other adverbs, and adjectives.

Adversative - ἐναντιωματικός, ἡ, όν (A.D., *Conj.*) Apollonius Dyscolus, *On Conjunctions* 251.3
> Having the characteristics of expressing opposition or contrast.

Affirmative - κατηγορικός, ἡ, όν (Arist., *APr.*) Aristotle, *Anterior Analytics* 26a18
> Having the characteristics of agreement with a remark or request.

Affix (prefix, infix, suffix) - μόριον, τό (*EM*) *Etymologicum Magnum* / *Great Etymological Lexicon* 141.47
> A morphological element placed at the front of, in the middle of, or at the end of a word (or word's root or stem).

Agreement - σύνοδος, ἡ (A.D., *Synt.*) Apollonius Dyscolus, *On Syntax* 28.11
> The subject and verb agree in person, number, and gender.

Agreement in length/time units - ἰσόχρονος, ον, εῖν (A.D., *Synt.*) Apollonius Dyscolus, *On Syntax* 272.23
> Characteristic of a one line of a poem contains the same amount of syllables as another line of a poem.

Agreement in number - ἰσάριθμος, α, ον (A.D., *Synt.*) Apollonius Dyscolus, *On Syntax* 170.13

Characteristic of an instance when a subject is singular and
its matching pronoun is also singular.

Agreement, analogy - ἀκολουθία, ἡ (D.H., *Amm.*) Dionysius
Halicarnassensis, *Letter to Ammaeum* 2.2; (A.D., *Pron.*)
Apollonius Dyscolus, *On Pronouns* 2.24
    The subject and verb agree in person, number, and gender.

Alliterative - παρηχητικός, ἡ, όν (Eust.) Eustathius 452.4
    Having the characteristics of alliteration.

Alphabet - ἀλφάβητος, ὁ (*An. Bachm.* or *AB*) *Anecdota Graeca
/ Greek Anecdotes* 181
    In English, a group of ordered letters such as A, B, C (in
    Greek, A, B, Γ).

Alphabet, records - γράμματα, τά (Pl., *Cra.*) Plato, *Cratylus*
390e
    In English, a group of ordered letters such as A, B, C (in
    Greek, A, B, Γ).

Ambiguous word, ambiguity - ἀμφιβολία, ἡ (A.D., *Synt.*)
Apollonius Dsyscolus, *On Syntax* 311.10
    A word that often has more than one sense or meaning and
    is open to various interpretations.

Analogous, analogical - ἀκόλουθος, ον (A.D., *Pron.*)
Apollonius Dyscolus, *On Pronouns* 11.21
    When one thing is similar or comparable to another thing.

Analogous, analogical - ἀναλογητικός, ἡ, όν (A.D., *Conj.*)
Apollonius Dyscolus, *On Conjunctions* 241.14
    When one thing is similar or comparable to another thing.

Analogy - ἀναλογία, ἡ (A.D., *Synt.*) Apollonius Dyscolus, *On Syntax* 36.23

A comparison of one thing to another.

Analysis - ἀνάλυσις, ἡ (Arist., *EN.*) Aristotle, *Nichomachean Ethics* 1112b23

Parsing a complex idea into smaller portions so as to understand it with more clarity.

Analyzed element, solution to a problem - διάλυσις, ἡ (A.D., *Synt.*) Apollonius Dyscolus, *On Syntax* 243.11

Having been examined carefully and methodically, often leading to the resolution of a problem.

Anaphora, repetition - ἀναφορά, ἡ (Longin.) Longinus 20.1

To say or write more than once.

Anastrophe, inversion - ἀναστροφή, ἡ (A.D., *Synt.*) Apollonius Dyscolus, *On Syntax* 308.15

To place the verb before the subject.

Antiphrasis (word used in a sense opposite of its common meaning) - ἀντίφρασις, ἡ (Trypho, *Trop.*)

Trypho, *On Tropes* 2.15

When a word is used to convey its opposite meaning, often ironically. For instance, in English the "driveway" is where cars park, not drive.

Antistrophe, inversion of letters, or repetition of a sound or word (usually at the end of a line or sentence) - ἀντιστροφή, ἡ (Eust.) Eustathius 945.60; (EM) *Etymologicum Magnum / Great Etymological Lexicon* 424.8

Interchanging stanzas in a Greek choral ode.

Antistrophic - ἀντίστροφος, ον (Arist., *Pr.*) Aristotle, *Problems* 918b27

    Characteristic of interchanging stanzas in a Greek choral ode.

Antithesis - ἀντίθεσις, ἡ (Arist., *Rhet.*) Aristotle, *Rhetoric* 1410a22

    An opposing or contrasting idea that is parallel to another idea. For example, black/white, wrong/right, etc.

Aorist - συντελικός, τό (Phryn., *PS.*) Phrynicus, *Sophistic Preparations* 315

    A verb form that denotes the past tense without suggesting whether what took place in the past was habitual or has ongoing effects.

Aorist (tense) - ἀόριστος, ὁ (A.D., *Synt.*) Apollonius Dyscolus, *On Syntax* 276.5

    A verb form that denotes the past tense without suggesting whether what took place in the past tense was habitual or has ongoing effects.

Aorist subjunctive - αὐθυπότακτος, ον (Hdn., *Epim.*) Herodianus, *Partitions* 278

    The subjunctive form of the aorist is suggestive of something that will happen if the proper conditions are met or fulfilled.

Aoristic, completed - συντελικός, ἡ, όν (A.D., *Synt.*) Apollonius Dyscolus, *On Syntax* 70.9

    Having the characteristics of being related to the aorist tense.

Apodosis - ἀπόδοσις, ἡ (D.H., *Th.*) Dionysius Halicarnassensis, *On Thucydides* 52

The "then" part of an "if/then" conditional statement.

Apostrophe, elision - ἀποστροφή, ἡ (A.D., *Pron.*) Apollonius
Dyscolus, *On Pronouns* 46.1
In Greek when ἀλλά is followed by a word that begins
with a vowel and becomes ἀλλ' (thus the final alpha is
removed).

Appellation, common noun - προσηγορία, ἡ (D.T., *Ars gram.*)
Dionysius Thrax, *Art of Grammar* 634.6
Either the act of giving a name or title, or the name or title
itself.

Art, skill, method, system - τέχνη, ἡ (Arist., *Rh.*) Aristotle,
Rhetoric 1354a11
The art or system of grammar or rhetoric or logic.

Article - ἄρθρον, τό (Arist., *Rh.Al.*) Aristotle, *Rhetorica ad
Alexandrum* 1435a35
The word "the."

Articular - ἀρθρικός, ή, όν (A.D., *Synt.*) Apollonius Dyscolus,
On Syntax 6.5
Having the characteristics of the article or accompanying
the article.

Articular - σύναρθρος, ον (A.D., *Pron.*) Apollonius Dyscolus,
On Pronouns 13.6
Having the characteristics of being related to the article.

Aspirate - πνεῦμα, τό (A.D., *Adv.*) Apollonius Dyscolus, *On
Adverbs* 147.18
A word where the "h" sound is pronounced before a
vowel or vowel pair (diphthong).

Aspirated - δασύς, εῖα, ύ (D.T., *Ars gram.*) Dionysius Thrax,
Art of Grammar 631.22
> Often characteristic of a word or syllable having the "h"
> sound particularly before a vowel or vowel pair
> (diphthong).

Aspiration - πρόσπνευσις, ἡ (Phld., *Po.*) Philodemus, *On
Poems* 2.5
> Often understood as the act of pronouncing the "h" sound
> particularly before a vowel or vowel pair (diphthong).

Augment - αὔξησις, ἡ (*EM*) *Etymologicum Magnum* / *Great
Etymological Lexicon* 338.47
> The vowel prefixed to the front of Greek words which
> denotes "past tense" or "past time."

B

Bad grammar/syntax - κακοσυνταξία, ἡ (Eust.) Eustathius 210.29

    A writing or speech, for example, that contains and/or is characteristic of grammatical or syntactical errors.

Barbarism, foreign word - βαρβαρισμός, ὁ (A.D., *Synt.*) Apollonius Dyscolus, *On Syntax* 198.7

    In the ancient world, barbaric speech was often understood as non-Greek speech. A barbarism could also denote a misspelled, mispronounced or foreign (non-Greek) word.

Barytone (not oxytone) - βαρύτονος, ωενεῖν (A.D., *Pron.*) Apollonius Dyscolus, *On Pronouns* 35.25

    A word not having the acute accent on the last syllable.

Base form, root, radical - θέμα, τό (A.D., *Pron.*) Apollonius Dyscolus, *On Pronouns* 11.21

    The part of a word that does not change and to which affixes are added.

Book, scroll - βίβλος, ἡ (Phil., *Abr.*) Philo, *About Abraham* 1.9

    A collection of writings.

Bookish (related to books) - βιβλιακός, ἡ, όν (Porph., *Abst.*) Porphyrius Tyrius, *On Abstinence*, 47

    Having the characteristic of being related to books.

C

Calligraphy - εὐγραμματία, ἡ (Gal., *Capt.*) Galen, *On Language and Ambiguity* 14.587
> A style or form of writing that is often described as visually pleasing and artistic.

Case - πτῶσις, ἡ (Arist., *SE.*) Aristotle, *Sophistic Refutations* 173b27
> A grammatical system, usually denoted by inflection, that relates substantives to the other words in a sentence.

Catachresis (mixed metaphor) - κατάχρησις, ἡ (D.H., *Comp.*) Dionysius Halicarnassensis, *On Word Order* 3
> The purposeful misuse of a word often for dramatic effect.

Catalog, list - κατάλογος, ὁ (Pl., *Tht.*) Plato, *Theaetetus* 175a
> A list of items such as people, goods, places, etc.

Categorical, declarative - ἀποφαντικός, ἡ, όν (Arist., *Int.*) Aristotle, *On Interpretation* 17a8
> Having the characteristics of being put in a category or of a statement (as opposed to a command or question).

Causal - αἰτιολογικός, ἡ, όν (A.D., *Conj.*, *Adv.*) Apollonius Dyscolus, *On Conjunctions* 231.4, *On Adverbs* 200.2
> Expressive of the relationship between two actions or events. For example, cause and effect.

Causal - αἰτιώδης, ες (Chrysipp., *Stoic.*) Chrysippus, *Stoicism* 2.70
> Expressive of the relationship between two actions or events. For example, cause and effect.

Causal (conjunction) - αἰτιολογικός, ή, όν (A.D., *Conj.*; *Adv.*)
Apollonius Dyscolus, *On Conjunctions* 231.4, *On Adverbs* 200.2
    A conjunction that express a "cause." For example,
    "because."

Changed case - μετάκλισις, ή (Eust.) Eustathius 15.29
    When the case or case ending of a word is changed.

Chapter - κεφάλαιον, τό (Chor., in *Herm.*) Choricius, in *Hermes*
17.223
    A prominent division in a book.

Characteristic (of) - χαρακτηριστικός, ή, όν (A.D., *Synt.*)
Apollonius Dyscolus, *On Syntax* 103.17
    A trait belonging to a person or thing.

Chiasm - χιασμός, ὁ (Hermog., *Inv.*) Hermogenes, *On the
Invention of Arguments* 4.3
    A device that forms an AB / BA pattern thus giving a
    nice parallel or symmetrical effect.

Circumflex (accent) - περίκλασις, ή (D.T., *Ars gram.*)
Dionysius Thrax, *Art of Grammar* 630.2
    The (˜) mark or symbol placed over a letter to indicate a
    change in pitch or sound.

Circumflex (accent) - περισπωμένη, ή (A.D., *Pron.*) Apollonius
Dyscolus, *On Pronouns* 93.17
    The (˜) mark or symbol placed over a letter to indicate a
    change in pitch or sound.

Classification, parsed word (or sentence) - μερισμός, ὁ (A.D.,
Synt.) Apollonius Dyscolus, *On Syntax* 23.8, 140.11
    The arranging of items or parts of items or items or

parts that have been arranged.

Clause - κῶλον, τό (Arist., *Rhet.*) Aristotle, *Rhetoric* 1409b13
A grammatical category that consists of a subject and predicate but which may be independent or dependent.

Clumsiness (of language) - δυσκίνητος, ον (Pl., *R.*) Plato, *Republic* 503d
Something said or written in such a way that is grammatically questionable.

Collection (of laws, writings, etc.) - συναγωγή, ἡ (Arist., *EN.*) Aristotle, *Nichomachean Ethics* 1181b7
A group of words or texts.

Collective (w/nouns), copulative (w/conjunctions) - ἀθροιστικός, ἡ, όν (A.D., *Synt.*, *Conj.*) Apollonius Dyscolus, *On Syntax* 42.24, *On Conjunctions* 230.20
A collective term such as "nouns" or "eyes," etc.

Colon, comma - ὑποστιγμή, ἡ (D.T., *Ars gram.*) Dionysius Thrax, *Art of Grammar* 630.14
A mark or action signifying a brief suspension of speech or writing.

Colon, semicolon (middle point) - μέση (στιγμή), ἡ (Arist., *Ph.*) Aristotle, *Physics* 220a17
A punctuation mark that indicates a short break or pause in a writing. Both the colon and semicolon are now denoted by the raised dot symbol (·) in Koine.

Column (in a writing), white space between columns - σελίς, ἡ (σελίδες) (Phan., *AP.*; Suid.) Phanias, 6.295 (see *Anthologia Graeca*); Suidas (N/A)
A vertical portion of a composition.

Column or stone bearing an inscription - κίων, ὁ (ἡ) (Ar., V.)
Aristophanes, *Vespae Scholia* 105
> Many columns or stones in the ancient world had names or
> statements engraved on them, especially gravestones.

Comma, pause - διαστολή, ἡ (D.T., *Ars gram.*) Dionysius
Thrax, *Art of Grammar* 629
> A mark or action signifying a brief suspension of speech
> or writing.

Command - ἐντολή, ἡ (NT, *1 Ep. Cor.*) *1 Corinthians* 7.19
> An order given by an authoritative figure.

Comparative (of adverbs) - παραβολικός, ή, όν (Hom., *Il.*),
Homer, *Iliad* 13.2
> Having the characteristic of being comparable.

Comparative degree - συγκριτικός, ή, όν (A.D., *Synt.*)
Apollonius Dyscolus, *On Syntax* 58.28
> The comparative form of an adjective; a diminutive or
> superlative.

Comparison - σύγκρισις, ἡ (Arist., *Top.*) Aristotle, *Topics*
102b15
> The act of showing similar traits between two items.

Compound, complex - σύνθετος, η, ον (Aristo., *Po.*) Aristotle,
Poetics 1456b35
> Parts of a word or sentence joined to form a whole.

Compound, composite - διπλόος, η, ον (Arist., *Po.*) Aristotle,
Poetics 1459a9
> Parts of a word or sentence joined to form a whole.

Compound, composite - διπλοῦς, ῆ, οῦν (Arist., *Po.*) Aristotle, *Poetics* 1459a9

> Parts of a word or sentence joined to form a whole.

Conative - ὀρεκτικός, ἡ, όν (Arist., *EN.*) Aristotle, *Nichomachean Ethics* 1102b30

> Characteristic of expressing effort.

Concerned with the apodosis - ἀποδοτικός, ἡ, όν (*EM*) *Etymologicum Magnum / Great Etymological Lexicon* 763.8

> Having to do with the "then" part of an "if/then" statement.

Conditional / hypothetical conjunction - συναπτικός, ἡ, όν (A.D., *Conj.*) Apollonius Dyscolus, *On Conjunctions* 218.11

> Having the characteristics of requiring a condition to be met.

Conditional, hypothetical - ὑποθετικός, ἡ, όν (Arr., *Epict.*) Arrianus, *Writings on Epictetus* 1.7.22

> Having the characteristics of requiring a condition to be met.

Conjugated, joined - σύζυγος, ον (A.D., *Pron.*) Apollonius Dyscolus, *On Pronouns* 51.9

> Having the characteristic of being inflected with regard to items such as tense, voice, mood, etc.

Conjugation - συζυγία, ἡ (A.D., *Adv.*) Apollonius Dyscolus, *On Adverbs* 198.6

> The different forms of a word in light of grammatical categories such as tense, voice, mood, person, and number. A word that has been conjugated.

Conjunction - σύνδεσμος, ὁ (Arist., *Rh.*) Aristotle, *Rhetoric* 1407a20

A grammatical category whose words make connections between words, phrases, clauses, sentences, paragraphs, etc.

Conjunctive - συνδεσμικός, ή, όν (A.D., *Conj.*) Apollonius Dyscolus, *On Conjunctions* 235.5

Having the characteristics of or being related to a conjunction.

Conjunctive, connective - συνδετικός, ή, όν (A.D., *Synt.*) Apollonius Dyscolus, *On Syntax* 18.13

A word that connects other words, phrases, clauses, sentences, paragraphs, etc.

Connective, particle (causal) - παρασυναπτικός, ὁ (A.D., *Conj.*) Apollonius Dyscolus, *On Conjunctions* 220.14

A word that connects other words, phrases, clauses, sentences, paragraphs, etc.

Consonant - σύμφωνον, τό (A.D., *Pron.*) Apollonius Dyscolus, *On Pronouns* 11.2

Any letter that is not a vowel. In English, for example, "d," "g," "p," etc.

Consonants - ἄφωνα (γράμματα) (Pl., *Cra.*) Plato, *Cratylus* 393e

A letter that is not a vowel (e.g. d" or "n").

Construction (grammatical), combination - συνάρτησις, ή (A.D., *Synt.*) Apollonius Dyscolus, *On Syntax* 17.8

A construction or pattern related to grammar.

Contraction - περίστασις, ή (Vett.Val.) Vettius Valens 14.2

When a word form takes an affix or suffix without and as a result changes or morphs.

Contrast, comparison - ἀντιπαράθεσις, ἡ (A.D., *Synt.*)
Apollonius Dyscolus, *On Syntax* 49.21
    Different or similar traits between two items.

Copulative (conjunction) - συμπλεκτικός, ἡ, όν (A.D., *Adv.*)
Apollonius Dyscolus, *On Adverbs* 218.14
    A word that connects a subject and the predicate in a
    sentence.

Coronis (e.g. breathing mark) - κορωνίς, ἡ (*EM*) *Etymologicum
Magnum / Great Etymological Lexicon* 763.10
    The smooth breathing mark found in words such as ἐν.

Correct (spelling) - ὀρθογραφία, ἡ (A.D., *Adv.*) Apollonius
Dyscolus, *On Adverbs* 165.15
    A word that is written and spelled correctly.

Correct pronunciation, speaking - ὀρθοέπεια, ἡ (Pl., *Phdr.*)
Plato, *Phaedrus* 267c
    The speaking or pronouncing of a word or group of words
    clearly and correctly.

Correct speech or language - ὀρθολογία, ἡ (Pl., *Sph.*) Plato,
Sophists 239b
    A word that is spoken (or written) correctly.

Correction - διόρθωσις, ἡ (Arist., *SE.*) Aristotle, *Sophistic
Refutations* 176b34
    That which replaces a mistake.

Correlative - ἀνταποδοτικός, ή, όν (A.D., *Adv.*, *Conj.*)
Apollonius Dyscolus, *On Adverbs* 158.24, *On Conjunctions*
237.9
> One word that is connected to or has a relatioship with
> another word, i.e. "connective."

Crasis - κρᾶσις, ή (A.D., *Adv.*) Apollonius Dyscolus, *On
Adverbs* 128.2
> When two or more vowels merge. In Greek when the
> word ἐγώ follows the word καί (καὶ ἐγώ) they join to
> become the word κἀγώ.

Crasis, synaeresis, running together of sounds or words -
συναλιφή, ή (A.D., *Synt.*) Apollonius Dyscolus, *On Syntax*
140.14
> In Greek when the word ἐγώ follows the word καί (καὶ
> ἐγώ) they join to become the word κἀγώ.

Crasis, synaeresis, running together of sounds or words -
συναλοιφή, ή (A.D., *Synt.*) Apollonius Dyscolus, *On Syntax*
140.14
> In Greek when the word ἐγώ follows the word καί (καὶ
> ἐγώ) they join to become the word κἀγώ.

Crasis, to coalesce by crasis - κεράννυμι (D.H., *Comp.*)
Dionysius Halicarnassensis, *On Word Order* 22
> In Greek when the word ἐγώ follows the word καί (καὶ
> ἐγώ) they join to become the word κἀγώ.

D

Dative - δοτική, ἡ (A.D., *Synt.*) Apollonius Dyscolus, *On Syntax* 28.23

    The case that often denotes the indirect object in a sentence.

Dative - δοτικός, ή, όν (A.D., *Synt.*) Apollonius Dyscolus, *On Syntax* 28.23

    Characteristic of the case that often denotes the indirect object in a sentence.

Dative - ἐπισταλτικός, ή, όν (D.T., *Ars gram.*) Dionysius Thrax, *Art of Grammar* 636.6

    Characteristic of the case that often denotes the indirect object in a sentence.

Declarative, axiomatic - ἀξιωματικός, ή, όν (*Stoic.*) *Stoicorum Veterum Fragmenta / Old Stoic Fragments* 2.61

    Having the characteristic of a statement (as opposed to a command or question) or a true saying.

Declarative, explanatory, affirmative - διασαφητικός, ή, όν (A.D., *Conj.*) Apollonius Dyscolus, *On Conjunctions* 221.23

    Having the characteristic of a statement (as opposed to a command or question) or a true saying.

Definition - ἔννοια, ἡ (Hermog., *Prog.*) Hermogenes, *Progymnasmata* 6

    The meaning of a thought, concept, word, idea, etc.

Definition - ὅρος, ὁ (Chrysipp., *Stoic.*) Chrysippus, *Stoicism* 2.75

    The meaning of a thought, concept, word, idea, etc.

Degree (interval in rhythm) - βαθμός, ὁ (Iamb., *VP.*)
Iamblichus, *Life of Pythagorus* 26.120
> For example, the length between one syllable, word, or beat and the next.

Deliberative - συμβουλευτικός, ή, όν (Arist., *Rh.*) Aristotle, *Rhetoric* 1358b7
> Characteristic of speech having to do with politics or persuasion.

Demonstrative - ἀποδεικτικός, ή, όν (Arist., *APo.*) Aristotle, *Posterior Analytics* 74b10
> Characterisic of words such as pronouns and adjectives that point to specific things often making them definite. They are also referred to as "determiners."

Demonstrative - δεικτικός, ή, όν (A.D., *Pron.*) Apollonius Dyscolus, *On Pronouns* 5.19
> Characterisic of words such as pronouns and adjectives that point to specific things often making them definite. They are also referred to as "determiners."

Demonstrative (referent) - δεῖξις, ἡ (A.D., *Pron.*) Apollonius Dyscolus, *On Pronouns* 9.8
> Words such as pronouns and adjectives that point to specific things often making them definite. They are also referred to as "determiners."

Demonstrative pronoun - δεικτικὴ ἀντωνυμία, ἡ (A.D., *Pron.*) Apollonius Dyscolus, *On Pronouns* 9.17
> Words such as pronouns and adjectives that point to specific things often making them definite. They are also referred to as "determiners."

Deponent - ἀποθετικός, ή, όν (An. Bachm.) *Anecdota Graeca / Greek Anecdotes* 2.303, 2.304

> Verbs that are active in their meaning but take a passive or middle form.

Descriptive, narrative-like - διηγματικός, ή, όν (Arist., *Po.*) Aristotle, *Poetics*1459a17, 1459b36

> Having the characteristics of a detailed account or an account in general.

Difficult to inflect - δύσκλιτος, ον (*EM*) *Etymologicum Magnum / Great Etymological Lexicon* 763.8

> Characteristic of words having no inflections; in Greek the endings of many proper names do not change from case to case.

Difficult to say/pronounce - δυσεκφώνητος, ον (Eust.) Eustathius 76.33

> A word that is not easy to pronounce or say.

Digamma - δίγαμμα, τό (A.D., *Pron.*) Apollonius Dyscolus, *On Pronouns* 76.32

> The ancient Greek letter or symbol similar to the English "ϝ" that had a sound similar to "v."

Digression, close of a verse - ἐκβολή, ή (Philostr., *Her.*; Eust.) Philostratus, *The Heroic* 19.14; Eustathius 900.24

> An abrupt change of subject in the middle of a speech or writing.

Diminution - μείωσις, ή (Arist., *Cat.*) Aristotle, *Categories* 15a14

> The reducing or diminishing someone or something.

Diminutive - ὑποκοριστικός, ή, όν (D.T., *Ars gram.*) Dionysius
Thrax, *Art of Grammar* 634.25
>   Characteristic of a word or affix that denotes smallness.

Diphthong - δίφθογγον, τό (Hdn., *Epim.*) Herodianus,
Partitions 245
>   A pair of vowels that form one syllable.

Diphthong - δίφθογγος, ή (A.D., *Adv.*) Apollonius Dyscolus,
On Adverbs 128.8
>   A pair of vowels that form one syllable.

Direct (speech), correct (spelling) - ὀρθός, ή, όν (Pl., *Ti.*) Plato,
Timaeus 44b
>   Speech or discourse that is reports the actual words of the
>   speaker.

Direct Object - κατηγόρημα, τό (Arist., *Int.*) Aristotle, *On
Interpretation* 20b32
>   A noun (or noun phrase) that receives the action of the
>   verb directly from the subject.

Disjunctive - διαιρετικός, ή, όν (*Stoic.*) *Stoicorum Veterum
Fragmenta / Old Stoic Fragments* 2.87
>   A word that expresses a disconnect or contrast between
>   words, thoughts, ideas, etc.

Disyllabic - δισύλλαβος, ον (A.D., *Pron.*) Apollonius Dyscolus,
On Pronouns 49.14
>   Having the characteristic of having two syllables.

Division (of sections of a text) - παραγραφή, ή (Eust.)
Eustathius 107.46
>   A portion of a writing that is usually quite prominent.

Dual - διπρόσωπος, ον (A.D., *Pron.*) Apollonius Dyscolus, *On Pronouns* 17.1, 110.24

    Having the characteristics of being a pair.

Dual - δυϊκός, ή, όν (A.D., *Pron.*) Apollonius Dyscolus, *On Pronouns* 10.28

    Having the characteristics of being a pair.

E

Early grammar teacher - στοιχειωτής, ὁ (A.D., *Synt.*)
Apollonius Dyscolus, *On Syntax* 309.5
> Someone who teaches the basic principles or rules of
> grammar and speech to beginning learners.

Elementary/basic teaching - στοιχείωσις, ἡ (Phld., *Rh.*)
Philodemus, *Rhetoric* 1.104
> The principles or rules of grammar and speech taught at an
> early age.

Elements, sounds - στοιχεῖον, τό (A.D., *Synt.*) Apollonius
Dyscolus, *On Syntax* 313.7
> The basic building blocks of a word.

Elision - κουφισμός, ὁ (Eust.) Eustathius 150.24
> In Greek when ἀλλά is followed by a word that begins
> with a vowel and becomes ἀλλ' (thus the final alpha is
> removed).

Elision, apocope - ἀποκοπή, ἡ (A.D., *Synt.*) Apollonius
Dyscolus, *On Syntax* 6.11
> In Greek when ἀλλά is followed by a word that begins
> with a vowel and becomes ἀλλ' (thus the final alpha is
> removed).

Ellipse, ellipsis - ἔλλειψις, ἡ (A.D., *Synt.*) Apollonius Dyscolus,
On Syntax 117.19
> A grammatical feature that represents an omission. In
> English, the markings "…" denote ellipsis.

Elliptical - ἐκλειπτικός, ή, όν (Pall., in *Hp*.) Palladius, in
Hippocrates 2.145d
    Having the characteristics of ellipsis.

Emphasis - ἔμφασις, ή (Demetr., *Eloc*.) Demetrius Phalereus,
On Style 130
    Extra stress or significance upon a word or idea.

Emphasis - ἐπίτασις, ή (A.D., *Conj*.) Apollonius Dyscolus, *On
Conjunctions* 223.4
    The special importance or significance assigned to a word,
    idea, concept, etc.

Emphatic - ἐμφατικός, ή, όν (Demetr., *Eloc*.) Demetrius
Phalereus, *On Style* 68
    Having the characteristics of expressing emphasis.

Emphatic - καταφατικός, ή, όν (A.D., *Pron*.) Apollonius
Dyscolus, *On Pronouns* 49.11
    Having the characteristics of expressing emphasis.

Enclitic - ἐγερτικός, ή, όν (*An. Bachm*. or *AB*) *Anecdota
Graeca / Greek Anecdotes* 1147
    Having the characteristic of being an enclitic, that is, a
    second word that is usually pronounced as though it is
    connected to the first word. In Greek, this often occurs
    with personal pronouns that follow a word.

Enclitic - ἐγκλιτικός, ή, όν (A.D., *Synt*.) Apollonius Dyscolus,
On Syntax 222.22
    Having the characteristic of being an enclitic, that is, a
    second word that is usually pronounced as though it is
    connected to the first word. In Greek, this often occurs
    with personal pronouns that follow a word.

End (of a word or sentence) - τέλος, τό (A.D., *Pron.*)
Apollonius Dyscolus, *On Pronouns* 12.25
>That which is heard or seen at the end of a word or
>sentence; a case ending.

Ending (of a word) - προπαραλήγουσα, ἡ (A.D., *Pron.*)
Apollonius Dyscolus, *On Pronouns* 11.9
>A case ending or suffix.

Ending (of word or sentence) - λῆξις, ἡ (A.D., *Synt.*) Apollonius
Dyscolus, *On Syntax* 104.28
>The final part or portion of a word or sentence.

Ending (of word or sentence) - τελευτή, ἡ (Arist., *Rh.*) Aristotle,
Rhetoric 1420b2
>That which is heard or seen at the end of a word or
>sentence; a case ending.

Ending, penult - παραλήγουσα, ἡ (A.D., *Pron.*) Apollonius
Dyscolus, *On Pronouns* 11.9
>Either the last or next to last syllable of a word.

Epexegetical - ἐπεξηγηματικός, ή, όν (Pl., *Phd.*) Plato, *Phaedo*
64d
>Extra or additional words used that did not need to be
>used.

Epistle, letter - ἐπιστολή, ἡ (NT, *2 Ep. Cor.*) *2 Corinthians* 3.2
>A literary genre usually denoting letters but sometimes
>poems.

Etcetera - κτλ. (καὶ τὰ λοιπά) (Hyp., *Fr.*) Hyperides,
Fragments 162.2
>The ancient Greek equivalent of modern English's "etc."
>(Etcetera).

Etymological - ἐτυμολογικός, ή, όν (*EM*) *Etymologicum Magnum / Great Etymological Lexicon* 700.24
    Having the characteristics of etymology.

Etymology - ἐτυμηγορία, ή (See: ἐτυμολογία, ή)
    Either the origins or a word or the study of the origins of a word.

Etymology - ἐτυμολογία, ή (A.D., *Adv.*) Apollonius Dyscolus, *On Adverbs* 153.13
    Either the origins or a word or the study of the origins of a word.

Euphonic, euphonious - εὔφωνος, ον (Demetr., *Eloc.*) Demetrius Phalereus, *On Style* 70
    Having the characteristic of sounding good or pleasing.

Euphony - εὐφωνία, ή (Demetr., *Eloc.*) Demetrius Phalereus, *On Style* 68
    The pleasantness or agreeableness of sound.

Euphony - καλλιφωνία, ή (D.T., *Ars gram.*) Dionysius Thrax, *Art of Grammar* 675.14
    The pleasantness or agreeableness of sound.

Examination, exam - ἐξέτασις, ή (Pl., *Ap.*) Plato, *Apology* 22e
    For example, a test or quiz. Also a detailed review of someone or something.

Exegesis, explanation, interpretation - ἐξήγησις, ή (Pl., *Lg.*) Plato, *Laws* 631a
    The act of drawing meaning out of a text or speech and carefully interpreting its meaning.

Exegete, interpreter, commentator - ἐξηγηγτής, ὁ (Pl., *Euthphr.*) Plato, *Euthyphro* 4d, 9a
> Someone who practices the acts of exegesis and interpretation.

Exercise, practice - ἄσκησις, ἡ (Hp., *VM*) Hippocrates, *On Ancient Medicine* 4
> An exam or quiz.

Exhortation - παρακέλευσις, ἡ (Phld., *Oec.*) Philodemus, *On Economics* 36J
> A moral instruction or teaching.

Explanation - ἀνάπτυξις, ἡ (Arist., *Rh.Al.*) Aristotle, *Rhetorica ad Alexandrum* 1.1a
> Answer or statement given to describe or clarify a matter.

Expletive (conjunction or particle) - παραπληρωματικός, ὁ (A.D., *Conj.*) Apollonius Dyscolus, *On Conjunctions* 247.22
> An oath or curse/swear word.

F

Feminine - θηλυκός, ή, όν (A.D., *Synt.*) Apollonius Dyscolus,
On Syntax 222.6
> Having the characteristics of being feminine.

Feminine - θηλυπρεπής, ές (Dam., *Pr.*) Damascius, *On
Principles* 192
> Having the characteristics of being feminine.

Feminine - θηλύς, εῖα, ύ (Arist., *Po.*) Aristotle, *Poetics* 1458a10
> Having the characteristics of being feminine.

Final (letter or word) - τελικός (D.T., *Ars gram.*) Dionysius
Thrax, *Art of Grammar* 632.9
> Characteristic of that which is heard or seen at the end of
> a word or sentence; a case ending.

Form, long syllable - θέσις, ή (D.T., *Ars gram.*) Dionysius
Thrax, *Art of Grammar* 632.30
> In English the syllable "ee" in the word "feet" is long. In
> the Greek word λόγου the syllable "ου" is long.

Form, type, pattern, text, rough draft - τύπος, ὁ (A.D., *Synt.*;
Anon. in Phot., *Bibl.*) Apollonius Dyscolus, *On Syntax* 278.25;
Anonymous in Photius, *Bibliography* 491b
> A particular aspect, detail, or pattern related to a speech or
> composition.

From a compound - παρασύνθετος, η, ον (A.D., *Synt.*)
Apollonius Dyscolus, *On Syntax* 330.5
> A word derived from a compound word, for example, the
> word "otolaryngology."

Future (tense) - μέλλων, ὁ (Pi., *O.*) Pindar, *Olympian Odes* 10.7
    A verb tense that anticipates a state or action that will
    occur (in the future).

G

Gender - γένος, τό (Arist., *Rhet.*) Aristotle, *Rhetoric* 1407b7
Linguistic category that identifies whether a word is
masculine, feminine, or neuter.

Gender - φύσις, ἡ (Ar., *Lys.*) Aristophanes, *Lysistrata Scholia*
92
Linguistic category that identifies whether a word is
masculine, feminine, or neuter.

Gendered words marked by different endings - ἐκκόπτω (A.D.,
Synt.) Apollonius Dyscolus, *On Syntax* 104.23
When substantives express different gender based on their
endings.

Genitive - γενική, ἡ (D.T., *Ars gram.*) Dionysius Thrax, *Art of*
Grammar 636
A grammatical category that usually indicates possession
but can also indicate source, measure, etc.

Genitive - γενικός, ἡ, όν (D.T., *Ars gram.*) Dionysius Thrax,
Art of Grammar 636
Characteristic of a grammatical category that usually
indicates possession but can also indicate source,
measure, etc.

Genitive - πατρικός, ἡ, όν (Choerob., in Theod.) Choerboscus,
cited in Theodorus 1.111 H (see *Anthologia Graeca*)
A characteristic that usually indicates possession but can
also indicate source, measure, etc.

Grammar - γραμματική, ἡ (Pl., *Cra.*) Plato, *Cratylus* 431e

The system and structure of a language.

Grammar expert - γραμματιστής, ὁ (X., *Smp.*) Xenophon, *Symposium* 4.17
    Someone who has mastered the art and rules of grammar.

Grammar rule - κανόνισμα, τό (Eust.) Eustathius 439.26
    A principle or law governing the use of grammar.

Grammarian - γραμματικός, ὁ (Clem.Al., *Strom.*) Clement of Alexandria, *Stromata* (Or: *Miscellanies*) 1.16.79
    Someone who practices the art and rules of grammar.

Grammatical form - σχῆμα, τό (A.D., *Pron.*) Apollonius Dyscolus, *On Pronouns* 17.25
    A particular aspect, detail, or pattern related to grammar.

Grave (accent) - βαρύς, ὁ (Pl., *Cra.*) Plato, *Cratylus* 399b
    A mark (`) used to denote a pitch drop on a syllable.

Grave (accent) - βαρύτης, ἡ (Arist., *Po.*) Aristotle, *Poetics* 1456b33
    A mark (`) used to denote a pitch drop on a syllable.

Group, collection - ἄθροισις, ἡ (Porph., *Abst.*) Porphyrius Tyrius, *On Abstinence*, 1.29
    A group of words or texts.

H

Half-pronounced - ἡμίφωνος, ον (Aristaenet.) Aristaenetus 1.10
    Having the characteristic of not being fully pronounced.

Having five cases - πεντάπτωτος, ον (Priscian., *Inst.*)
Priscianus, *Institutes* 5.76
    Characteristic of a verb that is said to have the
    nominative, genitive, dative, accusative, and vocative
    cases.

Having to do with breathing(s) - πνευματικός, ή, όν (Arist.,
GA.) Aristotle, *Animal Species* 781a31
    For instance, the rough or smooth breathing marks
    (' or ').

Having two cases or endings - δίπτωτος, ον (A.D., *Pron.*)
Apollonius Dyscolus, *On Pronouns* 91.7
    A word that is characteristic of having two case endings.

Hissing sound (of a letter such as a sibilant) - συριγμός, ὁ (D.H.,
Comp.) Dionysius Halicarnassensis, *On Word Order* 14
    Usually heard in words containing s, x, or z. In Greek σ,
    ζ, or ξ.

Historical (e.g. present tense verb) - ἱστορικός, ή, όν (Arist.,
Po.) Aristotle, *Poetics* 1451b1
    Having to do with or concerning history. The use of a
    present tense verb to describe a state or event related to the
    past.

Homophone - ὁμοφωνία, ἡ (Arist., *Pol.*) Aristotle, *Politics*
1263b35

A word that has the same pronunciation as another word
but a different meaning. For example "two" and "to."

Hortatory - παραινετικός, ή, όν (AristoStoic.) Aristo Chius,
1.80
> Having the characteristics of a moral instruction or
> teaching.

Hortatory - παρακελευσματικός, ή, όν (Eust.) Eustathius
1393.4
> Having the characteristics of a moral instruction or
> teaching.

Hypallage (reversal of two syntactically related words) -
ὑπαλλαγή, ἡ (A.D., *Synt.*) Apollonius Dyscolus, *On Syntax*
209.6
> An inversion of word order for dramatic effect as with
> hyperbaton. This is often found in Dr. Seuss books.

Dyscolus, *On Syntax* 209.6
> An inversion of word order for dramatic effect as with
> hyperbaton. This is often found in Dr. Seuss books.

Hyperbatonic (transposed words or clauses) - ὑπερβατός, ή, όν
(Arist., *Rh.Al.*) Aristotle, *Rhetoric to Alexander* 1438a28
> An interruption of normal word order for dramatic effect.
> This is very prominent in poetry.

I

Illiterate, inarticulate - ἀγράμματος, ον (Pl., *Ti.*) Plato, *Timaeus* 23a

> Unable to read, write, or speak.

Imperfect (of tense) - παράτασις, ἡ (A.D., *Synt.*) Apollonius Dyscolus, *On Syntax* 70.27

> Denoting the state or action of a verb that occurred in the past and whose action or state was either incomplete or durative.

Imperfect (tense) - παρατατικός, ὁ (A.D., *Synt.*) Apollonius Dyscolus, *On Syntax* 10.19

> Denoting the state or action of a verb that occurred in the past and whose action or state was either incomplete or durative.

Impersonal (verb) - ἀπρόσωπος, ον (Phld., *Lib.*) Philodemus, *On Bold Speech* 29O

> Characteristic of a verb that has no specific subject. For example, in the sentence "It is clear." there is no specific or determinate subject.

Improperly used words or phrases - ἄκυρος, ον (Cic., *Fam.*) Cicero, *Letters to Friends* 16.17.1

> When a word is used incorrectly, for example, a slang term or solecism. In English, "a'int" is typically understood as "improper."

Inarticulate - ἀσαφής, ές (Arist., *Aud.*) Aristotle, *On Sounds* (Or: *On Things Heard*) 801b21

> The inability to speak properly.

Inchoative - ἐναρκτικός, ή, όν (*Lex.Vind.*) *Vindobonense Lexicon* 19.3 (ε)
> Denoting the beginning of verb's action.

Incorrect phrasing - ἀκυρολεξία, ἡ (Eust.) Eustathius, 1770
> To improperly use a phrase or figure of speech, to mispronounce.

Incorrect phrasing - ἀκυρολογία, ἡ (D.H., *Lys.*) Dionysius Halicarnassensis, *On Lysias* 4
> To improperly use a phrase or figure of speech, to mispronounce.

Incorrectly (used) - ἀκυριολέκτητος, ον (Hermog., *Meth.*) Hermogenes, *On The Method of Effective Speech* 3
> Having the characterstic of being used incorrectly. For example, a slang term or solecism. In English, "a'int" is typically understood as "improper."

Incorrectly (used) - ἀκυρολέκτητος, ον (Hermog., *Meth.*) Hermogenes, *On The Method of Effective Speech* 3
> Having the characterstic of being used incorrectly. For example, a slang term or solecism. In English, "a'int" is typically understood as "improper."

Indeclinability - ἀκλισία, ἡ (A.D., *Pron.*) Apollonius Dyscolus, *On Pronouns* 12.4
> Incapable of being inflected.

Indeclinable - ἄκλιτος, ον (A.D., *Synt.*) Apollonius Dyscolus, *On Syntax* 30.10
> Lacking grammatical inflection. A word stays the same regardless of case. For example, in Greek the name Μιχαηλ (Michael).

Indeclinable - ἄπτωτος, ον (A.D., *Synt.*) Apollonius Dyscolus, *On Syntax* 176.5

> Having no inflections. In Greek, the endings of many proper names do not change from case to case.

Indeclinable - μονόκλιτος, ον (*EM*) *Etymologicum Magnum / Great Etymological Lexicon* 314.23

> Characteristic of a word that lacks grammatical inflection, that is, it stays the same regardless of case. For example, in Greek the name Μιχαηλ (Michael).

Indefinite article - ἀσύναρθρος, ον (A.D., *Synt.*) Apollonius Dyscolus, *On Syntax* 101.5

> Lacking the article. In English this may be represented by "a" or "an."

Indicative - ὁριστική, ἡ (A.D., *Synt.*) Apollonius Dyscolus, *On Syntax* 31.14

> Related to a verb expressing the reality or realness of a situation.

Indicative, finite - παρεμφατικός, ή, όν (A.D., *Pron.*; D.H., *Comp.*) Apollonius Dyscolus, *On Pronouns*; Halicarnassensis, *On Word Order* 5

> Related to a verb expressing the reality or realness of a situation.

Indivisible, inseparable - ἀμερής, ές (Arist., *APo.*) Aristotle, *Posterior Analytics* 100b2

> Having the characteristic of syllables such as "ea" in the word "conceal." As an inseparable syllable these vowels cannot be separated.

Inferential, illative - ἐπιφορητικός, ή, όν (A.D., *Conj.*)
Apollonius Dyscolus, *On Conjunctions* 258.16
>   Having the characteristics of an inference that has been
>   drawn.

Infinitive - ἀπαρέμφατος, ὁ (A.D., *Synt.*) Apollonius Dyscolus,
On Syntax 76.16, 2226.20
>   A verb form that acts and often functions like a
>   substantive.

Inflectable - πτωτικός, ή, όν (A.D., *Pron.*) Apollonius
Dyscolus, *On Pronouns* 9.5
>   Having the characteristic of being able to undergo
>   inflection.

Inflected form - ἔγκλιμα, τό (A.D., *Synt.*) Apollonius Dyscolus,
On Syntax 83.2
>   A word that has been altered by the addition of affixes (i.e.
>   prefixes, infixes, and suffixes).

Inflection - κίνημα, τό (Hdn., *Gr.*) Herodianus, *Prosody*
(*Herodiani Technici reliquiae*) 2.265
>   The act or process of changing the form of a word in order
>   to express a specific grammatical, idea, function, etc.

Inflection - κίνησις, ή (*EM*) *Etymologicum Magnum / Great
Etymological Lexicon* 220.37
>   The act or process of changing the form of a word in order
>   to express a specific grammatical concept, idea, function,
>   etc.

Inflection, augment - κλίσις, ή (A.D., *Pron.*; *EM*) Apollonius
Dyscolus, *On Pronouns* 12.14; *Etymologicum Magnum / Great
Etymological Lexicon* 23.53
>   The act of changing the form of a word in order to express

a specific grammatical concept, idea, function, etc.

Initial - ἀρκτικός, ή, όν (A.D., *Synt.*) Apollonius Dyscolus, *On Syntax* 28.19
> To be first or at the front of.

Ink - μέλαν, τό (Pl., *Phdr.*) Plato, *Phaedrus* 276c
> A liquid (usually dark) used for writing or similar activities.

Inseparable - ἀχώριστος, ον (Arist., *EN.*) Aristotle, *Nichomachaen Ethics* 1102a30
> The "ea" syllable in the word "conceal" is an inseparable syllable, i.e. these vowels cannot be separated.

Inseparable (syllable) - ἀδιάστατος, ον (A.D., *Pron.*) Apollonius Dyscolus, *On Pronouns* 86.21
> Having the characteristic of syllables such as "ea" in the word "conceal." As an inseparable syllable these vowels cannot be separated.

Insertion - ἔνθεσις, ή (Pl., *Cra.*) Plato, *Cratylus* 426c
> That which has been placed inside of something (e.g. a word) or in between something (e.g. letters or words).

Instrumental - ὀργανικόν, τό (Plu., *Cat.Mi.*) Plutarch, *Cato Minor* 4
> A word that functions as a means or agency. In Greek this often associated with the dative case.

Intensified, intensive - ἐπιτατικός, ή, όν (A.D., *Conj.*) Apollonius Dyscolus, *On Conjunctions* 223.4
> Having the characteristic of a word that is an intensifier or has been affected by an intensifier, that is, a word that has been more greatly emphasized.

Intensive - ἐπιτατικός, τό (Theoc., Sch.) Theocritus, *Scholia* (Or: *Scholastic Sayings*) OC632

An adjective, particle, or adverb that helps emphasize a thought, concept, idea, etc.

Interchangeable - διάλληλος, ον (A.D., *Adv.*) Apollonius Dyscolus, *On Adverbs* 126.2

When one block of information interchanges with another. For example, in a chiasm.

Interchanged form - ἀντιμετάληψις, ἡ (A.D., *Adv.*) Apollonius Dyscolus, *On Adverbs* 155.1

When one word can be spelled two different ways; or like a chiasm, where one block of information interchanges with another.

Interjection - ἀναφώνημα, τό (Heph., *Poëm.*) Hephaestio, *On Poems* 5.3

"Oh!" "No!" "Sorry!", for example.

Interjection - ἐπιφώνημα, τό (*An. Bachm.* or *AB*) *Anecdota Graeca / Greek Anecdotes* 100

An emphatic remark, such as an exclamation, that often begins, ends, or interrupts speech.

Interpolated - παρένθετος, ον (Eust.) Eustathius 67.29

Characteristic of a word or group of words inserted into a sentence, text, story, etc. (after its completion).

Interpolation - παρεμβάλη, ἡ (Alex.Aphr., in *Top.*) Alexander Aphrodisiensis, in *Topics* (by Aristotle) 309.27

A word or group of words inserted into a sentence, text, story, etc. (after its completion).

Interpretive, explanatory - ἑρμηνευτικός, ή, όν (Pl., *Plt.*.) Plato, *Politics* 260d
> Having the characteristics of being explained in detail.

Interrogatory - ἐρωτηματικός, ή, όν (Hermog., *Prog.*)
Hermogenes, *Progymnasmata* 3
> Having the characteristics of being a question.

Interrogatory - πυσματικός, ή, όν (A.D., *Pron.*) Apollonius
Dyscolus, *On Pronouns* 27.16
> Having the characteristics of being a question.

Interrogatory, interrogative - πευστικός, ή, όν (A.D., *Adv.*)
Apollonius Dyscolus, *On Adverbs* 193.26
> Having the characteristics of being a question.

Intransitive - ἀμετάβατος, η, ον (A.D., *Pron.*) Apollonius
Dyscolus, *On Pronouns* 44.12
> Characteristic of verbs that do not take a direct object.

Intransitive, self-ending - αὐτοτελής, ἑς (A.D., *Synt.*)
Apollonius Dyscolus, *On Syntax* 116.11
> A verb that has or takes no direct object.

Introduction - εἰσαγωγή, ή (D.H., *Amm.*) Dionysius
Halicarnassensis, *Letter to Ammaeum* 2.1
> The frontal or opening material of a writing or speech.

Irregular - παράλογος, ον (A.D., *Pron.*) Apollonius Dyscolus,
On Pronouns 27.26
> Characteristic of a deviation from standard usage or meaning.

Irregular, anomalous - ἀνακόλουθος, ον, ία (A.D., *Pron.*)
Apollonius Dyscolus, *On Pronouns* 66.1

A deviation from standard usage or meaning.

Irregular, inadmissible - ἀσύστατος, ον (A.D., *Pron.*)
Apollonius Dyscolus, *On Pronouns* 55.11
>   Having the characteristic of not being grammatically normative, sound, or correct.

Irregular, ungrammatical - ἀσύντακτος, ον (Choerob., in Theod.) Choerboscus, cited in Theodorus 18H see *Anthologia Graeca*)
>   Having the characteristic of not being grammatically normative, sound, or correct.

Isosyllabic (having balanced number of syllables) - ἰσοσύλλαβος, ον (A.D., *Pron.*) Apollonius Dyscolus, *On Pronouns* 11.8
>   Characteristic of an instance when one the amount of syllables in one word are the same as the amount of syllables in another word.

L

Lacking synaloepha (i.e. merging of two syllables into one) - ἀσυνάλειπτος, ον (Hdn., *Gr.*) Herodianus, *Prosody (Herodiani Technici reliquiae)* 2.912
> When two syllables are not merged into one but remain distinct.

Language, dialect - διάλεκτος, ἡ (Hdn., *Gr.*) Herodianus, *Prosody (Herodiani Technici reliquiae)* 2.932
> A system of speech and communication used to talk.

Language, dialect, foreign word - γλῶσσα, ἡ (γλῶττα) (Demetr., *Eloc.*) Demetrius Phalereus, *On Style* 177
> A system of speech and communication used to talk.

Length - μακρότης, ἡ (A.D., *Adv.*) Apollonius Dyscolus, *On Adverbs* 187.15
> The measurement of a syllable, vowel, etc.

Lesson, session - μάθημα, τό (Pl., *Smp.*) Plato, *Symposium* 211
> A period of time in which teaching occurs or the content of what is taught.

Letter - γράμμα, τό (A., *Pr.*) Aeschylus, *Prometheus* 460
> A symbol or character used to represent speech sounds.

Liquid consonant - εὐμάλακτος, ον (*EM*) *Etymologicum Magnum / Great Etymological Lexicon* 700.24
> A letter spoken without friction and which can be prolonged, such as "r" or "l" in English.

Liquified or nasalic - ὑγρός, ά, όν (D.T., *Ars gram.*) Dionysius Thrax, *Art of Grammar* 632.9

> Having the characteristics of or being related to a liquid or nasal.

Long syllable - μακρὰ συλλαβή (D.T., *Ars gram.*) Dionysius Thrax, *Art of Grammar* 17.4

> In English the syllable "ee" in the word "feet" is long. In the Greek word λόγου the syllable "ου" is long.

Long syllable (or vowel) - μακρός, ά, όν (Ar., *Av.*) Aristophanes, *Aves* 1131

> In English the syllable "ee" in the word "feet" is long. In the Greek word λόγου the syllable "ου" is long.

Lower case letters - μικρὰ γράμματα, τά (Arist., *Pr.*) Aristotle, *Problems* 958a35

> A written form of letters that is smaller than upper case letters. Often called miniscules.

M

Mark, note - ἐπισημασία, ἡ (Phld., *Rh.*) Philodemus, *Rhetoric* 1.12

A word or symbol used to draw attention to particular thoughts, ideas, or words.

Mark, note, sign - σημεῖον, τό (Heph., *Poëm.*) Hephaestio, *On Poems* 73c

A word or symbol used to draw attention to particular thoughts, ideas, or words.

Masculine - ἀρρενικός, ἡ, όν (Ph., *Leg.*) Philo, *On the Sacred Laws of Allegory* 1.294

A grammatical category whose words are often related to "male" persons or things but which also contains many words that, in terms of sexual gender, are arbitrary.

Masculine - ἀρσενικός, ἡ, όν (D.T., *Ars gram.*) Dionysius Thrax, *Art of Grammar*, 634.17

A grammatical category whose words are often related to "male" persons or things but which also contains many words that, in terms of sexual gender, are arbitrary.

Masculine - ἄρσην, ὁ (ἡ) (Ar., *Nu.*) Aristophanes, *Clouds* 682

A grammatical category whose words are often related to "male" persons or things but which also contains many words that, in terms of sexual gender, are arbitrary.

Maxim, anecdote - χρέια, ἡ (Hermog., *Prog.*) Hermogenes, *Progymnasmata* 3

A trustworthy saying or proposition.

Meaning - δύναμις, ἡ (Pl., *Cra.*) Plato, *Cratylus* 394b
 The thought, concept, idea, etc., that the subject intends to
 send or express to recipients.

Memory, inscription, record - μνήμη, ἡ (Arist., *Rh.*) Aristotle,
Rhetoric 1361a34
 Something from the past which has been written down or
 mentally remembered.

Metaphor - μεταφορά, ἡ (Arist., *Po.*) Aristotle, *Poetics* 1457b6
 Something that represents or symbolizes something else.

Metaphorical - μεταφορικός, ἡ, όν (Phld., *Po.*) Philodemus, *On
Poems* 2.55
 Having the characteristics of being a metaphor.

Metaplasm (sound change, synizesis) - συνίζησις, ἡ (*EM*)
Etymologicum Magnum / Great Etymological Lexicon 279.8
 The act of a word's spelling and sound undergoing change.

Meter - μέτρον, τό (Ar., *Nu.*) Aristophanes, *Clouds* 638
 The rhythm denoted by the structure of a writing.

Metonymy (one word used for another) - μετωνυμία, ἡ (Ps. -
Plu., *Vit.Hom.*) Pseudo-Plutarch, *Life of Homer* 23
 The act of using one word to represent another. For
 example, in English, the use of the word "pig" for "cop."

Middle - μέσον, η, ον (A.D., *Synt.*) Apollonius Dyscolus, *On
Syntax* 276.21
 Referring to the middle voice or, in general, something
 that is in the middle of or between other items.

Middle (voice) - μέση (διάθεσις), ἡ (*EM*) *Etymologicum
Magnum / Great Etymological Lexicon* 754.18

The action of the verb that is both carried and received by the subject.

Middle (voice) - μεσότης, ἡ (A.D., *Synt.*) Apollonius Dyscolus, *On Syntax* 211.19
> The action of the verb that is both carried and received by the subject.

Mistake, error - σφάλμα, τό (Pl., *Tht.*) Plato, *Theaetetus* 168a
> An incorrect portion of something spelled, written, or spoken.

Modified, inflected - ἐμπαθής, ἐς (A.D., *Synt.*) Apollonius Dyscolus, *On Syntax* 47.16
> To make partial changes to a word or word group which often convey extra details or meaning.

Monophthong (single vowel sound or syllable) - μονόφθογγος, ἡ (Theodos., *Can.*) Theodosius, *Canons (On Grammar)* 68H
> A single vowel or a single vowel sound.

Monosyllabic - μονοσύλλαβος, ον (A.D., *Pron.*) Apollonius Dyscolus, *On Pronouns* 27.2
> Having the characteristic of only having one syllable. For example, the English word "ah."

Mood, mode, change of acute to grave accent, inflection - ἔγκλισις, ἡ (A.D., *Synt.*, *Pron.*, *Adv.*; Dexipp., in *Cat.*) Apollonius Dyscolus, *On Syntax* 248.14, *On Pronouns* 8.7, *On Adverbs* 169.23; Dexippus in *Commentary on Aristotle's Categories* 33.8
> A grammatical category that denotes the reality of what the verb expresses (e.g. actuality, potentiality, etc.).

Mute, voiceless - ἄφθογγον, τό (Pl., *Philb.*) Plato, *Philebus* 18c, (Pl., *Cra.*) *Cratylus* 424c

A letter that causes a vocal stop and prevents further airflow (e.g. "t" or "d").

N

Nasal (velar) - ἄγμα, τό (Prisc., *Inst.*) Priscianus, *Institutes* 1.39
A letter spoken that allows air to escape through the nose, for example "m" or "n."

Negation - ἄρνησις, ἡ (D.T., *Ars gram.*) Dionysius Thrax, *Art of Grammar*, 642.3; (Lesb.) Lesbonax, 26
The act of making a word or statement negative.

Negative particle - ἀπορηματικός, ἡ, όν (A.D., *Conj.*) Apollonius Dyscolus, *On Conjunctions* 258.15
An element or word of speech that negates another word or sentence, such as οὐκ in Greek.

Negative particle - ἀποφατικός, ἡ, όν (A.D., *Synt.*) Apollonius Dyscolus, *On Syntax* 245.24
An element or word of speech that negates another word or sentence, such as οὐκ in Greek.

Neuter - αὐτουδέτερος, ον (An. Bachm.) *Anecdota Graeca / Greek Anecdotes* 2.302
Characteristic of words often related to "neuter" or "sexless" things; words that, in terms of sexual gender, are arbitrary.

Neuter - μεταξύ, τό (Arist., *Po.*) Aristotle, *Poetics* 1458a17
Words often related to "neuter" or "sexless" things; words that, in terms of sexual gender, are arbitrary.

Neuter - οὐδέτερος, ἡ, όν (A.D., *Pron.*) Apollonius Dyscolus, *On Pronouns* 6.19
Characteristic of words often related to "neuter" or "sexless" things; words that, in terms of sexual gender,

are arbitrary.

No ending - ἄληκτος, ον (Demetr. Lac., *Herc.*) Demetrius
Lacon, *Herculaneum Papyri* 1061.7
> A sentence or writing that seems very long or without
> ending.

Nominative - ὀνομαστικός, ή, όν (A.D., *Synt.*) Apollonius
Dyscolus, *On Syntax* 107.4
> A grammatical category usually denoting or pointing to
> the subject of the sentence.

Nominative - ὀρθή, ή (A.D., *Pron.*) Apollonius Dyscolus, *On
Pronouns* 6.19
> A grammatical category usually denoting or pointing to
> the subject of the sentence.

Non-barbaric - ἀβαρβάριστος, ον (*Lex. Vind.*) Lexicon
Vindobonense 294
> Proper and intelligible language or speech.

Non-doubled - ἀδιπλασίαστος, ον (Eust.) Eustathius, 781.15
> A single letter instead of a pair of letters. For example, or
> a non-reduplicated augment or stem.

Non-reflexive - ἀλλοπαθής, ές (A.D., *Pron.*, *Synt.*) Apollonius
Dyscolus, *On Pronouns* 44.17, *On Syntax* 175.13
> When the action of a subject is not placed or focused back
> upon itself.

Not having an apodosis - ἀνανταπόδοτος, ον (Ar., *Pl.*)
Aristophanes, *Plutus* 469
> A conditional sentence that lacks the "then" part of an
> "if/then" statement.

Not having an apodosis - ἀναπόδοτος, ον (Ar., *Av.*)
Aristophanes, *Aves* 7
> A conditional sentence that lacks the "then" part of an
> "if/then" statement.

Not in agreement - ἀδιαφορέω (A.D., *Pron.*) Apollonius
Dyscolus, *On Pronouns* 45.22, 68.15
> For example, when a subject and the verb do not agree
> with one another in a sentence.

Not in agreement - ἀκαταλληλία, ἡ (A.D., *Synt.*) Apollonius
Dyscolus, *On Syntax* 167.1
> For example, when a subject and the verb do not agree
> with one another in a sentence.

Notebook, tablet, parchment - μεμβράνα, ἡ (NT, *2 Ep. Ti.*) *2
Timothy* 4.13
> Material used to write words upon.

Noun, name, word - ὄνομα, τό (A.D., *Synt.*) Apollonius
Dyscolus, *On Syntax* 12.25
> A term that denotes a person, place, thing, or idea.

Number - ἀριθμός, ὁ (Secund., *Sent.*) Secundus, *Sentences* (Or:
Opinions) 4
> A mathematical symbol used to express an amount or to
> count. In grammar it refers to singularity and plurality.

Numerical - ἀριθημτικός, ἡ, όν (Arist., *EN.*) Aristotle,
Nichomachean Ethics 1106a35
> Having to do with number(s).

O

Oblique (case) - πλάγιος, α, ον (A.D., *Pron.*) Apollonius
Dyscolus, *On Pronouns* 23.1
>The genitive, dative, or accusative case. Any of the cases
>but the nominative and vocative cases.

Of a different case - ἀνομοιόπτωτος, ον (Eust.) Eustathius
1228.62
>Not of the same case (e.g. nominative, genitive, etc.).

Of a different ending - ἀνομοιοκατάληκτος, ον (A.D., *Synt.*)
Apollonius Dyscolus, *On Syntax* 167.25
>Not of the same case ending (e.g. nominative, genitive.,
>etc.).

Of a different gender - ἀνομοιογενής, ές (S., *Ant.*) Sophocles,
Antigone 74
>Not of the same gender (e.g. masculine, feminine, neuter).

Of two genders, of doubtful gender - διγενής, ές (Eust.)
Eustathius 150.27
>A word that is ambiguous in gender.

Omitted augment - ἀναυξησία, ἡ (Greg.Cor., *Trop.*) Gregorius
Corinthius, *On Tropes* 180
>In Greek when a past tense augment is omitted or left off
>of the front of a verb.

One unskilled in grammar or writing - ἰδιώτης, ὁ (Pl., *Phdr.*)
Plato, *Phaedrus* 258d
>Someone who cannot read, write, or speak accurately or
>articulately.

Onomatopoeia - ὀνοματοποιία, ἡ (Str., *Chr.*) Strabo,
Chrestomathy 14.2.28

>A word formed from the sound associated with it. For
>example the English words "moo" and "meow."

Optative - εὐκτικός, ή, όν (A.D., *Synt.*) Apollonius Dyscolus,
On Syntax 248.6

>A grammatical mode or mood used to indicate a desire,
>wish or hope.

Origin, derivation - παραγωγή, ἡ (A.D., *Synt.*) Apollonius
Dyscolus, *On Syntax* 192.3

>The point from which something, such as a word, came
>into existence.

P

Page, column of writing - σέλις, ἡ (Hsch.; LXX, *Je.*) Hesychius 383.1; *Jeremiah* 43 (36).23

> A portion of a writing or the material upon which a text is written.

Paper (papyrus - sheet/piece of) - χάρτης, ὁ (LXX, *Is.*) *Isaiah* 8.1

> Material used to write words upon.

Papyrus - πάπυρος, ὁ (ἡ) (Thephr., *HP.*) Theophrastus, *History of Plants* 4.8.2

> A substance from an Egyptian plant that is used to make a paper-like material for writing on. A document made of papyrus.

Parable, comparison - παραβολή, ἡ (NT, *Ev.Marc.*) *Mark* 12.1

> A story or similarity used to illustrate a point.

Paradigm, proof from example - παράδειγμα, τό (Arist., *Rh.*) Aristotle, *Rhetoric* 1393a27

> The common or usual pattern of how words and/or other grammatical entities form and function.

Paragraph, division that marks a change in speakers - παράγραφος, ὁ (Heph., *Poëm.*) Hephaestio, *On Poems* 5.3

> A prominent division in a chapter.

Parallel - παράλληλος, ον, ότης (A.D., *Adv.*) Apollonius Dyscolus, *On Adverbs* 140.13

> Characteristic of either lines of a writing that run side by side or are similar, or one thing that is similar or analogous

to another.

Paranesis (or: paraenesis), exhortation - παραίνεσις, ἡ (A., *Eu.*)
Aeschylus, *Eumenides* 707
> A moral instruction or teaching.

Parenthesis - μεσοσυλλαβία, ἡ (E., *Med.*) Euripedes, *Medea*
1085
> Either a pair of symbols or markings used to draw
> attention to or include a word or some other part of speech,
> or an insertion into a passage or thought that completes the
> passage or thought.

Parenthesis, interjection - παρένθεσις, ἡ (Hermog., *Id.*)
Hermogenes, *On Ideas* 1.12
> Either a pair of symbols or markings used to draw
> attention to or include a word or some other part of speech,
> or an insertion into a passage or thought that completes the
> passage or thought.

Part (of speech or word) - μέρος, τό (A.D., *Pron.*) Apollonius
Dyscolus, *On Pronouns* 4.6
> The grammatical category into which any word might fall.

Participial - μετοχικός, ἡ, όν (A.D., *Synt.*) Apollonius
Dyscolus, *On Syntax* 84.23
> Having the characteristics of being a participle.

Participle - μετοχή, ἡ (A.D., *Synt.*) Apollonius Dyscolus, *On
Syntax* 15.20
> A word formed from a verb and an adjective that functions
> as/like an adjective or complement.

Particle, epithet - προσθήκη, ἡ (Demetr., *Eloc.*) Demetrius
Phalereus, *On Style* 55

A particle is a word that does not inflect and which is usually very short. In English "not" is often considered a particle.

Parts of speech - τὰ μέρη τοῦ λόγου (A.D., *Pron.*) Apollonius Dyscolus, *On Pronouns* 18.5
>The categories to which words belong based on their syntactical functions.

Parts of speech - τὰ στοιχεῖα τῆς λέξεως (D.H., *Rh.*) Dionysius Halicarnassensis, *On Rhetoric* 7.2
>The categories to which words belong based on their syntactical functions.

Passive - παθητικός, ή, όν (A.D., *Synt.*) Apollonius Dyscolus, *On Syntax* 150.19
>Having the characteristics of being able to be acted upon.

Passive - πάθος, η, ον (A.D., *Synt.*) Apollonius Dyscolus, *On Syntax* 12.17
>Having the characteristics of being able to be acted upon.

Passive - ὕπτιος, α, ον (D.L.) Diogenes Laertius 7.43, 7.64
>Having the characteristics of being able to be acted upon.

Past (of the) - παροιχόμενος, η, ον (A.D., *Adv.*) Apollonius Dyscolus, *On Adverbs* 123.17
>Related to a verb expressing that something occurred in the past or in past time.

Pause, cadence, period - ἀνάπαυσις, ἡ (Hermog., *Id.*) Hermogenes, *On Ideas* 1.1
>A temporary stop or a repetitive rhythm often marked with the symbol (.).

Penultimate - παρατελευταῖος, α, ον (Ath.) Athenaeus 3.106c
    Characteristic of being placed on the next to last syllable
    of a word.

Penultimate - παρατέλευτος, ον (Ar., *Pl.*) Aristophanes, *Plutus*
598
    To be or to be placed on the next to last syllable of a word.

Perfect (tense) - παρακείμενος, ὁ (A.D., *Synt.*) Apollonius
Dyscolus, *On Syntax* 205.15
    A grammatical category denoting the state or action of a
    verb that occurred in the past and whose action or state
    was completed.

Perfect, complete - συντελής, ἡ (ὁ) (A.D., *Synt.*) Apollonius
Dyscolus, *On Syntax* 252.9
    Denoting the state or action of a verb that occurred in the
    past and whose action or state was completed.

Period (final mark/point) - περίοδος, ἡ (Heph., *Poëm.*)
Hephaestio, *On Poems* 3.5
    A temporary stop or a repetitive rhythm often marked
    with the symbol (.).

Personification, change of grammatical person - προσωποποιία,
ἡ (A.D., *Adv.*) Apollonius Dyscolus, *On Adverbs* 131.16
    The application of human characteristics to something that
    is not human.

Phonetic, vocal(ized) - φωνητικός, ἡ, όν (Porph., *Abst.*)
Porphyrius Tyrius, *On Abstinence*, 3.3
    Having the characteristic of being related to sound.

Phrase - φράσις, ἡ (Ar., *Nu.*) Aristophanes, *Clouds* 488
    A small collection or group of words that work together to

create a thought or idea.

Plagiarism, transposition, metathesis - μετάθεσις, ἡ (A.D., *Pron.*; Demetr., *Eloc.*) Apollonius Dyscolus, *On Pronouns* 51.5; Demetrius Phalereus, *On Style* 112
> The act of using someone's work or words as if they were your own. The act of changing letters (whether purposefully or not).

Pleonasm - πλεονασμός, ὁ (A.D., *Synt.*) Apollonius Dyscolus, *On Syntax* 267.14
> The act of using more words than are needed to make a point or convey meaning.

Pluperfect (tense) - ὑπερσυντελικός, ὁ (A.D., *Synt.*) Apollonius Dyscolus, *On Syntax* 281.6
> Denoting the state or action of a verb that started in the past, was repeated for a while, and whose action or state finally came to completion.

Plural - πληθυντικός, ἡ, όν (A.D., *Pron.*) Apollonius Dyscolus, *On Pronouns* 11.2
> Having the characteristic of not being single; having more than one.

Pluralization - πληθυσμός, ὁ (Dam., *Pr.*) Damascius, *On Principles* 53
> The act of making something plural.

Poem - ποίημα, τό (Pl., *Phd.*) Plato, *Phaedo* 60d
> A writing or speech that is often rhythmical, metaphorical, song-like, and contains rhyming words.

Poetic license - ἄδεια, ἡ (Him., *Or.*) Himerius, *Orations* 1.1; (A.D., *Pron.*) Apollonius Dyscolus, *On Pronons* 38.3, 69.19

Any instance when a speaker or writer disrupts the
expected order of speech or grammar to draw further
attention to what is being said.

Polysyllabic - πολυσύλλαβος, ον (D.H., *Comp.*) Dionysius
Halicarnassensis, *On Word Order* 11
Characteristic of having multiple syllables.

Possessive - οἰκειωματικός, ή, όν (*EM*) *Etymologicum
Magnum / Great Etymological Lexicon* 30.6
Characteristic of words that express ownership or
possession of someone or something.

Possessive (genitive) - κτητικός, ή, όν (A.D., *Pron.*) Apollonius
Dyscolus, *On Pronouns* 16.15
Expressing ownership or possession of someone or
something.

Possessive pronoun - κτητική ἀντωνυμία, ή (A.D., *Pron.*)
Apollonius Dyscolus, *On Pronouns* 101.18
A pronoun that expresses ownership or possession of
someone or something.

Possessive pronoun, with the article - σύναρθρος, ή (A.D.,
Pron.) Apollonius Dyscolus, *On Pronouns* 95.16
A pronoun that expresses ownership or possession of
someone or something.

Postposition, subordination - ὑπόταξις, ή (A.D., *Pron.*)
Apollonius Dyscolus, *On Pronouns* 116.5
A word or clause that is postpositive or subordinate.

Postpositive, subsidiary (of the pronoun αὐτός) -
ἐπιταγματικός, ή, όν (A.D., *Pron.*) Apollonius Dyscolus, *On
Pronouns* 45.12

A word that cannot come first in a sentence or an affix that cannot come first in a word.

Potential (of particles) - δυνητικός, ή, όν (A.D., *Synt.*)
Apollonius Dyscolus, *On Syntax* 10.28
Words that express possibility as opposed to actuality.

Prayer, wish, vow - εὐχή, ή (Hom, *Od.*) Homer, *Odyssey* 10.526
An activity used to express oneself with a deity.

Predicate - κατηγορούμενον, τό (Ar., *Fr.*) Aristophanes, *Fragments* 7.13
The part of a sentence that contains the verb and conveys information about the subject.

Prefix, prepositive - πρόταξις, ή (A.D., *Adv.*) Apollonius Dyscolus, *On Adverbs* 125.7
A word, letter, or group of words or letters placed before other words, letters, or groups of words or letters.

Preposition - πρόθεσις, ή (A.D., *Synt.*) Apollonius Dyscolus, *On Syntax* 305.24
A word that denotes a relationship between a noun or pronoun and other words in a sentence, clause, or phrase.

Prepositional - προθετικός, ή, όν (A.D., *Synt.*) Apollonius Dyscolus, *On Syntax* 305.24
Having the characteristics of being a preposition or being governed by a preposition.

Prepositive - προτακτικός, ή, όν (A.D., *Synt.*) Apollonius Dyscolus, *On Syntax* 306.15
Having the characteristics of a word, letter, or group of words or letters placed before other words, letters, or

groups of words or letters.

Present (tense) - ἐνεστώς, ὁ (A.D., *Pron.*) Apollonius Dyscolus, *On Pronouns* 58.7
>Expresses action or state of being at the time of speaking.

Present (tense) - παρών, οὖσα, ὄν (Pl., *Tht.*) Plato, *Theaetetus* 186b
>Related to a verb expressing the reality or realness of a situation.

Previous, prior, first - πρότερος, η, ον (Arist., *Pol.*) Aristotle, *Politics* 1316a16
>Something that came first in order, time, or significance.

Primary, prototypical - πρωτότυπος, ον (Dam., *Pr.*) Damascius, *On Principles* 340
>Characteristic of a first or original example or type which subsequent types are based on.

Principal - κεφάλαιος, α, ον (Ar., *Ra.*) Aristophanes, *Ranae* 854
>Having the characteristic of being first or highest in order of rank or importance.

Principal parts - θεματικόν, τό (A.D., *Adv.*) Apollonius Dyscolus, *On Adverbs* 121.5
>The forms of a verb from which its inflected forms can be realized.

Principal parts - πρῶτα μέρη, τά (D.H., *Comp.*) Dionysius Halicarnassensis, *On Word Order* 74-75
>The forms of a verb from which its inflected forms can be realized.

Prohibition - κώλυσις, ἡ (Arist., *Top.*) Aristotle, *Topics* 161a15

A command or law forbidding something.

Prolepsis - πρόληψις, ἡ (Hermog., *Meth.*) Hermogenes, *On The Method of Effective Speech* 10
>   Something spoken of (often anachronistically) before it happens (e.g. like a flash-forward).

Proleptic - προληπτικός, ἡ, όν (A.D., *Pron.*) Apollonius Dyscolus, *On Pronouns* 10.22
>   Having the characteristics of being proleptic (see πρόληψις, ἡ).

Prominent, vivid - σαφής, ές (Pl., *Prt.*) Plato, *Protagoras* 352a
>   Having the characteristic of being important or distinguished.

Pronomial - ἀντωνυμικός, ἡ, όν (A.D., *Synt.*) Apollonius Dyscolus, *On Syntax* 156.7
>   Characteristic of a pronoun.

Pronoun, antonym - ἀντωνυμία, ἡ (A.D., *Pron.*) Apollonius Dyscolus, *On Pronouns* 2.1
>   A word that substitutes for another word, which often prevents repetition. For example, words such as "he," "she," "it," etc.

Pronounce with a circumflex - περισπώμενος, η, ον (A.D., *Pron.*) Apollonius Dyscolus, *On Pronouns* 33.24
>   To raise the pitch of a word and then to immediately drop the pitch of a word.

Pronunciation - ἐκφορά, ἡ (D.H., *Comp.*) Dionysius Halicarnassensis, *On Word Order* 14
>   An enunciated or spoken sound.

Pronunciation - προφορά, ἡ (D.H., *Dem.*) Dionysius
Halicarnassensis, *On Demosthenes* 22
> An enunciated or spoken sound.

Proparoxytonic (acute accent on the antepenult) -
προπαροξυντικός, ἡ, όν (Eust.) Eustathius 75.37
> Having the characteristic of being or being on the
> antepenult.

Proparoxytonic (acute accent on the antepenult) -
προπαροξύτονος, ον (D.T., *Ars gram.*) Dionysius Thrax, *Art of
Grammar* 108 U
> Having the characteristic of being or being on the
> antepenult.

Proper (noun) - κύριος, α, ον (A.D., *Pron.*) Apollonius
Dyscolus, *On Pronouns* 10.11
> A name that identifies a noun (e.g. a person, place, etc.).

Properly, appropriate - ἰδίως (Dam., *Pr.*) Damascius, *On
Principles* 40
> Having the characteristics of being proper, right, or
> correct.

Proportionate - ἀνάλογος, ον (Arist., *EN.*) Aristotle,
Nichomachaen Ethics 1158a35
> Balanced or even. For example, syllables in a word or
> words in a sentence.

Prosaic (of prose) - πεζός, ἡ, όν (D.H., *Comp.*) Dionysius
Halicarnassensis, *On Word Order* 6
> Having the characteristics of being prose.

Prose author - συγγραφεύς, ὁ (Pl, *Phdr.*) Plato, *Phaedrus* 235c
> Someone who composes prose literature.

Protasis - πρότασις, ἡ (D.L.) Diogenes Laertius 3.52
    The "if" part of an "if/then" statement.

Punctuation mark - ἀνυπόκριτος, ὁ (D.T., *Ars gram.*) Dionysius
Thrax, *Art of Grammar* 24h
    Symbols or markings that denote the organization and
    intentions of a sentence.

Punctuation mark - νυγμή, ἡ (Plu., *Ant.*) Plutarch, *Antonius* 86
    Symbols or markings that denote the organization and
    intentions of a sentence.

Punctuation mark, period, colon - στιγμή, ἡ (D.T., *Ars gram.*)
Dionysius Thrax, *Art of Grammar* 630.6
    Symbols or markings that denote the organization and
    intentions of a sentence. A temporary stop or a repetitive
    rhythm often marked with the symbol (.).

Purpose - προαίρεσις, ἡ (Arist., *EN.*) Aristotle, *Nichomachean
Ethics* 1094a2
    The reason something is created, used, or done.

Q

Quantity - ποσός, ή, όν (Arist., *EN*.) Aristotle, *Nichomachean Ethics* 1158b31

    The amount or number of persons or things.

Question - ἐρώτημα, τό (Pl., *Prt*.) Plato, *Protagorus* 336d

    An expression used to ask for data or information about someone or something.

Question - πεῦσις, ή (D.H., *Dem*.) Dionysius Halicarnassensis, *On Demosthenes* 54

    An expression used to ask for data or information about someone or something.

Question, inquiry - ἀνάκρισις, ή (Pl., *Phdr*.) Plato, *Phaedrus* 277e

    An expression used to ask for data or information about someone or something.

R

Raised pitch/voice (with an acute accent) - ἀνάτασις, ἡ (D.T., *Ars gram.*) Dionysius Thrax, *Art of Grammar* 620.1
>   The raising of pitch when pronouncing a word with an acute accent.

Reciprocal, reflexive - ἀντανάκλαστος, ον (Prisc., *Inst.*) Priscianus, *Institutes* 11.1
>   Characteristic of subjects in a sentence that are able to direct the action of the verb back upon themselves (e.g. "myself").

Reciprocal, reflexive - ἀντιπεπονθώς, υῖα, ός (*Stoic.*) *Stoicorum Veterum Fragmenta / Old Stoic Fragments* 2.59
>   Characteristic of subjects in a sentence that are able to direct the action of the verb back upon themselves (e.g. "myself").

Reduplication - ἀναδίπλωσις, ἡ (Trypho, *Fr.*) Trypho, *Fragments* 12
>   When the stem or root of a word is repeated. For example, in Greek when the verb λανθάνω becomes λέληθεν in the perfect tense. (The λ is doubled.)

Reduplication - διπλασιασμός, ὁ (A.D., *Synt.*) Apollonius Dyscolus, *On Syntax* 323.6
>   When the stem or root of a word is repeated. For example, in Greek when the verb λανθάνω becomes λέληθεν in the perfect tense. (The λ is doubled.)

Referent - ἀπότασις, ἡ (A.D., *Synt.*) Apollonius Dyscolus, *On Syntax* 35.38

The person or thing to which an expression refers.

Reflexive - αὐτοπαθής, ἐς (A.D., *Pron.*) Apollonius Dyscolus,
On Pronouns 44.11
> Characteristic of subjects in a sentence that are able to
> direct the action of the verb back upon themselves (e.g.
> "myself").

Refuted, privative - ἀνατρεπτικός, ή, όν (Hermog., *Meth.*)
Hermogenes, *On The Method of Effective Speech* 10
> Something that has been proven erroneous or wrong.

Relative - ἀναφορικός, ή, όν (A.D., *Pron.*) Apollonius
Dyscolus, *On Pronouns* 5.20
> Having the characteristic of a pronoun that can function as
> a subject, object, or possessive pronoun (e.g. who, that,
> whose).

Relative pronoun - ἀναφορικὴ ἀντωνυμία, ή (Theodos., *Can.*)
Theodosius, *Canons (On Grammar)* 19.9
> A pronoun that can function as a subject, object, or
> possessive pronoun (e.g. who, that, whose).

Relative pronoun - ὑποτακτιὸν ἄρθρον, τό (Eust.) Eustathius
387.15
> A pronoun that can function as a subject, object, or
> possessive pronoun (e.g. who, that, whose).

Repetition - ἀναπόλησις, ή (A.D., *Synt.*) Apollonius Dyscolus,
On Syntax 29.10
> To be said or written more than once.

Resolution (of a diphthong into two syllables or one word into
two words) - διαίρεσις, ή (A.D., *Pron.*) Apollonius Dyscolus,
On Pronouns 87.2

When a pair of vowels are not merged into one syllable but remain distinct.

Retracted (accent) - βαρυντικός, ή, όν (*EM*) *Etymologicum Magnum / Great Etymological Lexicon* 763.8

> When an accent is thrown (leftward) back toward the front of a word.

Retraction (of an accent) - ἀνάδοσις, ή (*EM*) *Etymologicum Magnum / Great Etymological Lexicon* 549.30

> When an accent is thrown (leftward) back toward the front of a word.

Root - ῥίζα, ή (Pl., *Ti.*) Plato, *Timaeus* 81c

> The part of a word that does not change and to which affixes are added.

Rough (breathing) - δασύ, τό (A.D., *Synt.*) Apollonius Dyscolus, *On Syntax* 319.20

> Often understood as the "h" sound pronounced particularly before a vowel or vowel pair (diphthong).

Rule, paradigm - κανών, ὁ (A.D., *Adv.*) Apollonius Dyscolus, *On Adverbs* 141.25

> The common or usual pattern of how words and/or other grammatical entities form and function.

S

Scribe, scholar - γραμματεύς, ὁ (A., *Fr.*) Aeschylus, *Fragments* 358

Someone who practices the art of writing or composition.

Semicolon, colon - ἡ μέση στιγμή (D.T., *Ars gram.*) Dionysius Thrax, *Art of Grammar* 314.11

A punctuation mark that indicates a short break or pause in a writing.

Semi-vowel - ἡμίφωνον, τό (D.T., *Ars gram.*) Dionysius Thrax, *Art of Grammar* 631.16

The sound of a vowel or a vowel-like sound that functions as a consonant. In English, for example, the "y" in "yell" is said to function like a consonant.

Separation of vowel sounds or words - διάστασις, ἡ (A.D., *Pron.*) Apollonius Dyscolus, *On Pronouns* 87.4

An instance of epenthesis, i.e. an instance where a consonant may be inserted to separate vowels that do not belong together.

Short syllable - βραχεῖα συλλαβή (D.T., *Ars gram.*) Dionysius Thrax, *Art of Grammar* 631

A syllable containing a short vowel.

Short syllable or vowel - βραχύς, εῖα, ύ (D.T., *Ars gram.*) Dionysius Thrax, *Art of Grammar* 631

A word containing a short syllable or short vowel such as "bug" in English.

Significant (semantic) - σημαντικός, ή, όν (Arist., *Int.*)
Aristotle, *On Interpretation* 16a19
    Having the characteristic of carrying great importance.

Similar case, similar ending - ὁμοιόπτωτος, ον (A.D., *Synt.*)
Apollonius Dyscolus, *On Syntax* 124.26
    Characteristic of words whose case endings are similar.
    Characteristic of words whose endings are similar, usually
    in parallel lines of text.

Similarly ending, homoeoteleuton - ὁμοιοτέλευτος, ον (Phld.,
Rh.) Philodemus, *Rhetoric* 1.162
    Characteristic of words whose endings are similar, usually
    in parallel lines of text.

Similarly sounding - ὁμοιόφθογγος, ον (*EM*) *Etymologicum
Magnum / Great Etymological Lexicon* 169.10
    Characteristic of two or more words that contain the same
    sounds.

Similarly written, a forger - ὁμοιόγραφος, ον (A.D., *Conj.*;
Vett.Val.) Apollonius Dyscolus, *On Conjunctions* 258.14;
Vettius Valens 74.19
    Characteristic of a document, perhaps copied, that bears
    similarities to another document.

Singular - ἐνικός, ή, όν (A.D., *Pron.*) Apollonius Dyscolus, *On
Pronouns* 12.11
    Having the characteristic of being single.

Singular (of pronouns) - μονοπρόσωπος, ον (Hdn., *Gr.*)
Herodianus, *Prosody* (*Herodiani Technici reliquiae*) 2.26
    Having the characteristic of being single.

Small book, scroll - βιβλίον, τό (LXX, *1 Ma.*) *1 Maccabees*
12.9
> A small collection of writings.

Smooth (breathing) - ψιλόν, τό (A.D., Adv.) Apollonius
Dyscolus, On Adverbs 148.9
> The breathing mark found in words such as ἐν.

Smooth (breathing) - ψιλός, ή, όν (A.D., *Adv.*) Apollonius
Dyscolus, *On Adverbs* 148.9
> Characteristic of the smooth breathing mark which is
> found in words such as ἐν.

Solecism (grammatical error) - σολοικισμός, ὁ (A.D., *Synt.*)
Apollonius Dyscolus, *On Syntax* 198.8
> A word used incorrectly, for example, a slang term in
> speech or writing.

Sound - φθόγγος, ὁ (Ar., *Av.*) Aristophanes, *Aves* 1198
> Audible noises heard with the ear.

Sound - φωνή, ή (Pl., *Tht.*) Plato, *Theaetetus* 203b
> Audible noises heard with the ear.

Sound, breath, echo - ἦχος, ὁ (A.D., *Synt.*) Apollonius Dyscolus,
On Syntax 290.24
> Audible noises heard with the ear.

Specific - εἰδικός, ή, όν (A.D., *Synt.*) Apollonius Dyscolus, *On
Syntax* 230.11
> Having the characteristic of belonging to a particular
> category.

Speech, phrase, glossary - λέξις, ή (Arist., *Rhet.*) Aristotle,
Rhetoric 1406b1

A collection or group of words that work together to create a thought, idea, or reference guide.

Story, tale - διήγημα, τό (LXX, *Ezek.*) *Ezekiel* 17.2
An account of a series of events.

Style, form, letter, character - χαρακτήρ, ὁ (Hp., *Epid.*)
Hippocrates, *Epidemics* 3.1
The letters "b" or "c" or any other such character.

Style, form, something written - εἶδος, τό (*EM*) *Etymologicum Magnum / Great Etymological Lexicon* 763.8
A particular aspect, detail, or pattern related to a speech or composition.

Subject - ὑποκείμενον, τό (A.D., *Synt.*) Apollonius Dyscolus, *On Syntax* 122.17
A person, place, or thing denoting a state or action in a sentence.

Subject (of a writing) - ὑπόθεσις, ἡ (D.H., *Pomp.*) Dionysius Halicarnassensis, *Letter to Pompey* 3
A person, place, or thing being discussed in a writing.

Subjunctive - ὑποτακτικός, ἡ, όν (D.T., *Ars gram.*) Dionysius Thrax, *Art of Grammar* 638.8
Having the characteristic of the verbal mood in which is wished for, hoped for, or imagined.

Subscript (iota) - συγγραφόμενον, τό (D.T., *Ars gram.*) Dionysius Thrax, *Art of Grammar* 30
A letter or character written below another letter. In Greek the letter iota (ι) is often subscripted.

Subsequent - ὕστερος, α, ον (D.L.) Diogenes Laertius 7.10

Having the characteristic of being after something.

Substantive - ὑπαρκτικός, ή, όν (A.D., *Synt.*) Apollonius
Dyscolus, *On Syntax* 65.13
Having the characteristics of a noun or adjective.

Substantive with all three genders - τριγένεια, ή (A.D., *Synt.*)
Apollonius Dyscolus, *On Syntax* 212.23
And adjective that can be used across all three genders.

Superlative degree - ὑπερθετικός, ή, όν (A.D., *Adv.*)
Apollonius Dyscolus, *On Adverbs* 167.26
A type or form of an adjective that suggests the greatest or
least of something.

Syllable - συλλαβή, ή (Luc., *Jud. Voc.*) Lucianus, *The
Consonants at Law* 2.6
A group of letters having one vowel sound.

Symbolic - συμβολικός, ή, όν (Iamb., *VP.*) Iamblichus, *Life of
Pythagorus* 5.20
Having the characteristics of being a symbol or being
related to a symbol.

Synaeresis, contraction - συναίρεσις, ή (A.D., *Adv.*) Apollonius
Dyscolus, *On Adverbs* 132.25
The process of two adjacent vowels joining to become a
diphthong.

Syncope (loss of one or more letters in a word) - συγκοπή, ή
(A.D., *Adv.*) Apollonius Dyscolus, *On Adverbs* 169.15
The omission of letters or sounds in a word or phrase. For
example, in English, "'Sup?" for "What's up?"

Synonym - συνώνυμον, τό (A.D., *Synt.*) Apollonius Dyscolus, *On Syntax* 199.27

>A word that means the same thing as another word.

Synopsis - σύνοψις, ἡ (D.H., *Th.*) Dionysius Halicarnassensis, *On Thucydides* 6

>A side by side comparison of two or more items such as writings.

Synoptic - συνοπτικός, ἡ, όν (Pl., *R.*) Plato, *Republic* 537c

>Having the characteristics of being able to undergo a synopsis.

Syntactically well-formed - εὐσύντακτος, ον (Eust.) Eustathius 66.36

>Having the characteristic of proper syntax (sentence construction).

Syntactic element - σύνταγμα, τό (A.D., *Adv.*) Apollonius Dyscolus, *On Adverbs* 122.17

>A part or portion of a sentence.

Syntax - σύνταξις, ἡ (A.D., *Conj.*) Apollonius Dyscolus, *On Conjunctions* 214.7

>The arrangement of words and phrases to form sentences.

T

Table of contents, glossary - πίναξ[ι], ὁ (Plu., *Sull.*) Plutarch, *Sulla* 26

>A list of titles, chapters, or significant words located at either the front or back of a writing such as a book.

Tablet (wooden) πινακίδιον, τό (Plu., *Eum.*) Plutarch, *Eumenedes* 1

>Materials used for writing on. In antiquity tablets were made of various materials including wax, wood, stone, etc.

Temporal - καιρικός, ή, όν (Eust.) Eustathius 17.3

>Having the characteristic of being related to time or tense.

Temporal - χρονικός, ή, όν (A.D., *Pron.*) Apollonius Dyscolus, *On Pronouns* 15.24

>Having the characteristic of dealing with time.

Tense, time - χρόνος, ὁ (A.D., *Adv.*) Apollonius Dyscolus, *On Adverbs* 123.17

>Referring to an event or situation in time.

Terminal - ληκτικός, ή, όν (A.D., *Synt.*) Apollonius Dyscolus, *On Syntax* 7.10

>Having the characteristic of being the final part or portion of a word or sentence.

Thing, item, matter, affair - χρῆμα, τό (Hes., *Op.*) Hesiod, *Works and Days* 344, 402

>An object or event.

Thought - νόημα, τό (Pi., *P.*) Pindar, *Pythian Odes* 6.29

A mental or intellectual result or product of thinking.

Thought, meaning - διάνοια, ἡ (Pl., *Sph.*) Plato, *Sophists* 263d
A mental or intellectual result or product of thinking.

Title - τίτλος, ὁ (Just., *Nov.*) Justinianus, *Novels* 29.4
The name given to a composition.

To accentuate (place an accent upon) - τονόω (PS. -Zonar., *Lex.*)
Pseudo-Zonaras, *Lexicon* "ταυ" 1739.3
To place an accent on the antepenult, penult, or ultima.

To acquire meaning through context - συσσημαίνω (A.D., *Synt.*)
Apollonius Dyscolus, *On Syntax* 9.16
To figure out what a word means based on the context in
which it is used.

To aspirate - δασύνω (A.D., *Pron.*) Apollonius Dyscolus, *On
Pronouns* 12.21
Often understood as the act of pronouncing the "h" sound
particularly before a vowel or vowel pair (diphthong).

To be a grammarian - γραμματικεύομαι (Pall.) Palladius (see
Anthologia Graeca) AP9.169
Someone who practices the art and rules of grammar.

To be definite - ἀντιδιαστέλλω (A.D., *Synt.*) Apollonius
Dyscolus, *On Syntax* 37.7
The be the opposite of indefinite or ambiguous; often
marked by the definite article "the."

To be in error - διαπίπτω (Arr., *Epict.*) Arrianus, *Writings on
Epictetus* 2.22.36
To make a mistake spelling, writing, or speaking.

To be penultimate - παραλήγω (A.D., *Synt.*) Apollonius
Dyscolus, *On Syntax* 255.5
> To be or to be placed on the next to last syllable of a word.

To be reflexive - ἀντανακλάω (A.D., *Synt.*, *Pron.*) Apollonius
Dyscolus, *On Syntax* 175.12, *On Pronouns* 28.3
> When the subjects of a sentence are able to direct the
> action of the verb back upon themselves (e.g. "myself").

To change dialect, translate - μεταλαμβάνω (A.D., *Synt.*)
Apollonius Dyscolus, *On Syntax* 107.2
> To render words from one language into another.

To change final acute accent to grave - κοιμίζω (D.T., *Ars
gram.*) Dionysius Thrax, *Art of Grammar* 23
> καὶ instead of καί.

To change in form - μετασύρω (Eust.) Eustathius 32.42
> To add affixes to a root or stem can change the verb's
> form.

To cite - παραλέγω (Aen. Tact.) Aeneas Tacticus 4.7
> To identify a source of a quotation or proof.

To compare - ἀντιπαραβάλλω (Pl., *Hp.Mi.*) Plato, *Hippias
Minor* 369c
> To show similar traits between two items.

To compare - εἰκάζω (Arist., *EN.*) Aristotle, *Nichomachean
Ethics* 1106b30
> To show similar traits between two items.

To compare, combine - συγκρίνω (Arist., *Rh.*) Aristotle,
Rhetoric 1368a21
> The show similar traits between two items. The act of

joining two items.

To complete (a document) - πληρόω (Lyd., *Mag.*) Lydus, *On Roman Magistrates* 3.11
> To complete a writing such as a book.

To conjugate - κανονίζω (Opp., *Sch.*) Oppianus Anazarbensis, *Scholia* H.1.259
> To give different forms of a word in light of grammatical categories such as tense, voice, mood, person, and number.

To construct/write a diphthong - διφθογγίζω (Eust.) Eustathius 1571.29
> The act of writing a vowel pair in Greek such as ου.

To copy, transcribe - μεταγράφω (Luc., *Ind.*) Lucianus, *Against Indoctum* 4
> To duplicate a thought, comment, idea, etc. To render words from one language into another.

To correct - κατορθόω (Ph., *Leg.*) Philo, *On the Sacred Laws of Allegory* 1.124
> To fix an error or fault.

To correspond to (letters) - ἀντιστοιχέω (*EM*) Etymologicum Magnum / *Great Etymological Lexicon* 443.17
> When aspirated or unaspirated sounds correspond to certain letters. For example, the hissing sound corresponds to the letter sigma.

To decline - συγκλίνω (A.D., *Synt.*) Apollonius Dyscolus, *On Syntax* 102.11
> To analyze a word in order to figure out its declension.

To define - ὁρίζω (Pl., *Chrm.*) Plato, *Charmides* 171a
> To explain the meaning of a thought, concept, word, idea, etc.

To determine arbitrarily (a meaning or gender of a word) - θεματίζω (S.E., *M.*) Sextus Empiricus, *Against Mathematicians* 1.149, 1.152, 8.202
> Attempting to determine a gender for a non-gendered object.

To elide, drop out - ἐκθλίβω (A.D., *Conj.*) Apollonius Dyscolus, *On Conjunctions* 228.17
> In Greek when ἀλλά is followed by a word that begins with a vowel and becomes ἀλλ' (thus the final alpha is removed).

To elide, remove letters or words, to subtract - ἀφαιρέω (Pl., *Plt.*.) Plato, *Politics* 262d
> In Greek when ἀλλά is followed by a word that begins with a vowel and becomes ἀλλ' (thus the final alpha is removed).

To etymologize (trace a word's origins) - ἐτυμολογέω (*EM*) *Etymologicum Magnum / Great Etymological Lexicon* 220.37
> The act of tracing the origins of a word.

To feminize - ἐκθηλύνω (*EM*) *Etymologicum Magnum / Great Etymological Lexicon* 473.35
> To make something have the characteristics of being feminine.

To feminize - θηλύνω (Vett.Val.) Vettius Valens 76.6
> To make something have the characteristics of being feminine.

To follow (logically) - ἀκολουθέω (Pl., *Phd.*) Plato, *Phaedo*
1499a1007b; (Hermog. Id.) Hermogenes, *On Ideas* 400e
> When, in a conditional sentence the protasis ("if")
> is followed by the apodosis ("then"), giving us an
> "if/then" statement.

To form, derive, refer to - ἀνάγω (A.D., *Synt.*) Apollonius
Dyscolus, *On Syntax* 266.13
> To form a word or sentence from various grammatical
> parts.

To govern the subjunctive - ὑποτάσσω (*EM*) *Etymologicum
Magnum / Great Etymological Lexicon* 471.16
> To bring into conformity with the usage of the subjunctive
> mood.

To identify or signify the predicate - κατηγορέω (Arist., *Top.*)
Aristotle, *Topics* 140b37
> To point out, for example, that in the sentence "Michael
> sings." the predicate is "sings."

To indicate - ἐμφαίνω (D.S.) Diodorus Siculus 1.87
> To denote or point out.

To inflect - κλίνω (A.D., *Synt.*) Apollonius Dyscolus, *On Syntax*
212.20
> The act or process of changing the form of a word in order
> to express a specific grammatical concept, idea, function,
> etc.

To inflect, pronounce as an enclitic, or pronounce with the grave
accent - ἐγκλίνω (A.D., *Synt.*) Apollonius Dyscolus, *On Syntax*
120.10
> To change the form of a word in order to express a specific
> grammatical concept, idea, function,

etc.

To insert into the middle - μεσάζομαι (A.D., *Synt.*) Apollonius Dyscolus, *On Syntax* 270.5
> To place or put one or more items between other items.

To interpolate - παρεντίθημι (Hermog., *Id.*) Hermogenes, *On Ideas* 2.10
> To insert a word or group of words inserted into a sentence, text, story, etc. (after its completion).

To interpret - ἐξηγέομαι (Pl., *Cra.*) Plato, *Cratylus* 407a
> To carefully draw meaning out of and explain a text or speech.

To invert - ἀντιστρέφω (A.D., *Synt.*) Apollonius Dyscolus, *On Syntax* 180.16
> To turn inward, upside down, or in reverse order.

To invert order (e.g. words or accents) - ἀναστρέφω (Demetr., *Eloc.*) Demetrius Phalereus, *On Style* 11
> To place the verb before the subject.

To learn, understand - μανθάνω (Pl., *Euthd.*) Plato, *Euthydemus* 277e
> To acquire information, data, knowledge, or skill in something that has been taught.

To lengthen - μακρύνω (Nic., *Ep.*) Nicolaus I, *Epistles* 30.47
> To lengthen the sound of a vowel often through augmentation, that is, the addition of letters (esp. vowels) on to the front of a root or stem.

To lengthen - μεγεθύνω (A.D., *Adv.*) Apollonius Dyscolus, *On Adverbs* 193.23

To lengthen the sound of a vowel often through augmentation, that is, the addition of letters (esp. vowels) on to the front of a root or stem.

To lengthen or augment - ἐκτείνω (A.D., *Pron.*) Apollonius Dyscolus, *On Pronouns* 27.2
> To lengthen the sound of a vowel often through augmentation, that is, the addition of letters (esp. vowels) on to the front of a root or stem.

To make definite, pronounce - διαστέλλω (A.D., *Synt.*) Apollonius Dyscolus, *On Syntax* 37.7
> To make the opposite of indefinite or ambiguous, which is often achieved by using the definite article "the"; or to pronounce a word.

To make proparoxytonic - προπαροξύνω (A.D., *Pron.*) Apollonius Dyscolus, *On Pronouns* 30.7
> To place an accent on the antepenult.

To mean - δύναμαι (Ar., *Fr.*) Aristophanes, *Fragments* 691
> To signify, denote, or convey some type of thought, concept, idea, etc.

To paraphrase, translate - μεταφράζω (Plu., *Cat.Ma.*) Plutarch, *Cato Major* 19
> To restate an idea using different words. To render words from one language into another.

To parse (break into parts) - ἀναμερίζω (A.D., *Synt.*) Apollonius Dyscolus, *On Syntax* 114.3
> To break down a word or idea into smaller portions so as to understand it with more clarity.

To place in brackets - περιγράφω (Demonic.) Demonicus 1.3

To place a word or statement in brackets.

To prefix, make prepositive - προτάσσω (A.D., *Pron.*)
Apollonius Dyscolus, *On Pronouns* 116.6
>   To place a letter or word before another letter or word.

To pronounce - ἐκφέρω (D.H., *Comp.*) Dionysius
Halicarnassensis, *On Word Order* 15
>   To enunciate or speak a sound.

To Pronounce - ἐκφονέω (D.H., *Comp.*) Dionysius
Halicarnassensis, *On Word Order* 14
>   To enunciate or speak a sound.

To pronounce or speak correctly - ὀρθολογέω (Plu., *Mor.*)
Plutarch, *Moralia* 2.570e
>   To speak or pronounce a word or group of words clearly
>   and correctly.

To pronounce or speak pleasantly/beautifully - καλλιφωνέω
(Phld., *Rh.*) Philodemus, *Rhetoric* 1.176
>   To utilize euphony in speech.

To pronounce with an acute accent - ὀξύνω (A.D., *Pron.*)
Apollonius Dyscolus, *On Pronouns* 35.10
>   To raise the pitch when pronouncing a word with an
>   acute accent.

To pronounce with rough breathing - προσπνέω (A.D., *Pron.*)
Apollonius Dyscolus, *On Pronouns* 55.23
>   To pronounce the "h" sound particularly before a vowel
>   or vowel pair (diphthong).

To pronounce without accents - βαρύνω (A.D., *Synt.*) Apollonius
Dyscolus, *On Syntax* 120.4

To say a word without inflection, pitch, or accent change, that is, to say the word in a monotone manner.

To punctuate - περιστίζω (*EM*) *Etymologicum Magnum / Great Etymological Lexicon* 169.37
> To use symbols or markings in a writing to denote the organization and intentions of a sentence.

To punctuate - στίζω (Herm., in *Phdr.*) Hermias Alexandrinus in *Phaedrus* 84a
> To use symbols or markings in a writing to denote the organization and intentions of a sentence.

To raise in pitch, to intensify - ἐπιτείνω (Phld., *Po.*) Philodemus, *On Poems* 2.18
> Having the characteristic of being spoken with great acuteness.

To read, interpret - ἀναγινώσκω (Pi., *O.*) Pindar, *Olympian Odes* 10.1
> Usually the act of decoding and understanding written characters or symbols.

To refer to - ἀποτείνω (Luc., *Nigr.*) Lucianus, *Nigrinus* 13
> To speak of a person, place, thing, idea, etc.

To refute - ἀνατρέπω (Ar., *Nu.*) Aristophanes, *Clouds* 901
> To prove something erroneous or wrong.

To repeat - ἀναπολέω (Pi., *N.*) Pindar, *Nemean Odes* 7.104
> To say or write more than once.

To repeat - ἀναφέρω (Pl., *Ti.*) Plato, *Timaeus* 26a
> To say or write more than once.

To retract an accent (throw an accent backward) - ἀναβιβάζω
(A.D., *Pron.*, *Synt.*) Apollonius Dyscolus, *On Pronouns* 49.15,
On Syntax, 308.10
> When an accent is thrown (leftward) back toward the front
> of a word.

To retract, throw an accent backward - ἀναπέμπω (Hdn., *Gr.*)
Herodianus, *Prosody* (*Herodiani Technici reliquiae*) 278
> When an accent is thrown (leftward) back toward the front
> of a word.

To shorten - βραχύνω (Pl., *Per.*) Plutarch, *Pericles* 4
> To modify a long syllable into a short one.

To speak incorrectly - ἀκυρολογέω (*Lex. Vind.*) *Lexicon
Vindobonense* 3.19
> To improperly use a phrase or figure of speech, to
> mispronounce.

To understand - ὑπολαμβάνω (Pl., *Prt.*) Plato, *Protagoras* 341b
> To comprehend the meaning of an idea.

To understand a concept (even when a word is omitted) -
ὑπακούω (A.D., *Synt.*) Apollonius Dyscolus, *On Syntax* 22.21
> To comprehend the meaning of an idea.

To use a metaphor / metaphorically- μεταφέρω (Arist., *EN.*)
Aristotle, *Nichomachean Ethics* 1167a10
> To make one thing represent or symbolize another thing.

To use a pleonasm (extra words), to be redundant - πλεονάζω
(*EM*) *Etymologicum Magnum* / *Great Etymological Lexicon*
84.18
> To use more words than are needed to make a point or
> convey meaning.

To use a solecism (make a grammatical error) - σολοικίζω
(A.D., *Synt.*) Apollonius Dyscolus, *On Syntax* 199.14
> To use an incorrect word or to use a word incorrectly.

To use barbaric speech (i.e. unGreek speech) - βαρβαρίζω (Pl.,
Tht.) Plato, *Theaetetus* 175d
> In the ancient world, this was often understood as the act
> of using non-Greek speech or words.

To write an iota - ἰωτογραφέω (Ar., *V.*) Aristophanes, *Vespae
Scholia* 926
> To write the Greek letter iota (ι).

To write grammar rules - τεχνογραφέω (Phld., *Rh.*) Philodemus,
Rhetoric 1.170
> For example, in a grammar textbook.

To write next to, interpolate - παρεγγράφω (Aeschin., *Ep.*)
Aeschines, *Epistles* 3.74
> To insert a word or group of words inserted into a
> sentence, text, story, etc. (after its completion).

Top of a letter (of the alphabet) - κεραία, ἡ (A.D., *Synt.*)
Apollonius Dyscolus, *On Syntax* 28.27
> The peak of the letter "A."

Transitive - διαβατικός, ἡ, όν (A.D., *Synt.*) Apollonius
Dyscolus, *On Syntax* 43.18
> Characteristic of verbs that take a direct object.

Transitive - διαβιβαστικός, ἡ, όν (A.D., *Synt.*) Apollonius
Dyscolus, *On Syntax* 298.15
> Characteristic of verbs that take a direct object.

Transitive - μεταβατικός, ή, όν (A.D., *Pron.*) Apollonius Dyscolus, *On Pronouns* 24.15
>Having the characteristics of being transitive.

Transitively - ἀλλοπαθῶς (Eust.) Eustathius, 920.27
>Characteristic of verbs that take a direct object.

Transitivity - διάβασις, ή (A.D., *Synt.*) Apollonius Dyscolus, *On Syntax* 202.7
>Referring to a verb that is able to transfer action to the direct object.

Translation - μετάφρασις, ή (Plu., *Dem.*) Plutarch, *On Demosthenes* 2.347
>That which is rendered from one language into another.

Translation, interpretation - ἑρμηνεία, ή (Pl., *R.*) Plato, *Republic* 524b
>That which is rendered from one language into another or that which is explained in detail.

Transposed letter used to help form another word - ἀναγραμματισμός, ό (Eust.) Eustathius 45
>An anagram. For example, where the letters in the word "great" can be inverted to spell "retag."

Treatise - πραγματεία, ή (Arist., *Top.*) Aristotle, *Topics* 100a18
>A composition that focuses on a specific subject.

Triphthong - τρίφθογγος, ή (Tz., *H.*) Joannes Tzetzes, The Chiliades (Or: *Book of Histories*) 12.242
>A joining of three vowels that become pronounced as one syllable.

U

Unaccented - ἄτονος, ον (Emp., *Sphaer.*) Empedocles, *Sphere* 1.141
> A word lacking an accent or change in pitch.

Unambiguous - ἀναμφίβολος, ον (Ascl., *Tact.*) Asclepiodotus, *Tacitus* 12.11
> Incapable of being interpreted or understood more than one way.

Unapproved, unconvincing - ἀδόκιμος, ον (Ph., *Bel.*) Philo Mechanicus, *Excerpts*76.47
> The use of ungrammatical speech or forms, or when an argument or speech is not convincing.

Uncontracted - ἀσυναίρετος, ον (Eust) Eustathius 50.36
> When a word form takes an affix or suffix without contracting or morphing.

Undistinguished - ἀδιάστολος, ον (A.D., *Pron.*) Apollonius Dyscolus, *On Pronouns* 11.26
> When a word's case or gender may not be defined or recognizable.

Undistinguished - ἀδιαχώριστος, ον (*EM*) *Etymologicum Magnum / Great Etymological Lexicon* 538.34
> When a word's case or gender may not be defined or recognizable.

Unencliticized - ἀνέγκλιτος, ον (A.D., *Synt.*) Apollonius Dyscolus, *On Syntax* 136.7
> Characteristic of not receiving the effects of an enclitic.

Ungrammatical, grammar error - ἀσυνταξία, ἡ (A.D., *Pron.*, *Synt.*) Apollonius Dyscolus, *On Pronouns* 14.3, *On Syntax* 304.24

    A misspelling or some similar grammatical problem.

Ungrammatical, not in agreement - ἀκατάλληλος, ον (A.D., *Synt.*) Apollonius Dyscolus, *On Syntax* 30.5

    When a word is used incorrectly, for example, a slang term or solecism. In English, "a'int" is typically understood as "improper."

Uninflected - ἀδιάπταιστος, ον (*EM*) *Etymologicum Magnum / Great Etymological Lexicon* 643.47

    Having no inflections. In Greek, the endings of many proper names do not change from case to case.

Uninflected - ἀδιάπτωτος, ον (*EM*) *Etymologicum Magnum / Great Etymological Lexicon* 643.47

    Having no inflections. In Greek, the endings of many proper names do not change from case to case.

Uninflected - ἀμετάβλητος, ον (A.D., *Synt.*) Apollonius Dyscolus, *On Syntax* 322.26

    Having no inflections. In Greek, the endings of many proper names do not change from case to case.

Uninflected - ἀμετάθετος, ον (A.D., *Synt.*) Apollonius Dyscolus, *On Syntax* 322.1

    Words that have no inflections. In Greek, the endings of many proper names do not change from case to case.

Unpleasant sounding - δυσήκοος, ον (Demetr., *Eloc.*) Demetrius Phalereus, *On Style* 48

    The opposite of euphonic; the use of barbaric words,

speech, or sounds.

Unpleasant sounding - δύσφωνος, ον (Demetr., *Eloc.*) Demetrius
Phalereus, *On Style* 69
> The opposite of euphonic; the use of barbaric words,
> speech, or sounds.

Unpleasant sounding - κακόφωνος, ον (Arist., *Aud.*) Aristotle,
On Sounds (Or: *On Things Heard*) 802b23
> The opposite of euphonic; the use of barbaric words,
> speech, or sounds.

Unpronounced (letters) - ἀνεκφώνητος, ον (*EM*) *Etymologicum
Magnum / Great Etymological Lexicon* 203.7
> For example, in Greek, the iota subscript.

Unpunctuated writing - ἀστιξία, ἡ (*An. Ox.*) *Anecdota Graeca /
Greek Anecdotes* 4.51
> When a writing or speech lacks punctuation.

Unrhythmical (syllables) - ἄλογος, ον (D.H., *Comp.*) Dionysius
Halicarnassensis, *On Word Order* 20
> Unequal in measures of syllables.

Unskilled - ἰδιωτικός, ἡ, όν (Arist., *Po.*) Aristotle, *Poetics*
1458a21
> Characteristic of someone or something that lacks a
> specific set of skills or qualities.

V

Variant, variation - ἐξαλλαγή, ἡ (Procl., *Inst.*) Proclus,
Theological Institutes 162, 175
>A form of something that differs in one or more respects
>from a form of something else (that is usually similar).

Verb, sentence, predicate - ῥῆμα, τό (Pl., *Sph.*, *Cra.*; Arist., *Int.*)
Plato, *Sophists* 262a, Cratylus 399b; Aristotle, *On Interpretation*
16b6
>A grammatical category whose words denote an action or
>state of being. The part of a sentence containing the verb.

Verbal - ῥηματικός, ή, όν (A.D., *Adv.*) Apollonius Dyscolus,
On Adverbs 135.14
>Having the characteristics of being related to a verb.

Verse, line (of a writing), chapter - στίχος, ὁ (Heph., *Poëm.*)
Hephaestio, *On Poems* 1
>Typically a small portion of a writing.

Vertical line of a letter (of the alphabet) - κιονηδόν (D.T., *Ars
gram.*) Dionysius Thrax, *Art of Grammar* 183, 191
>Like a line made when writing a capital iota (I).

Vocative - κλητική, ἡ (D.T., *Ars gram.*) Dionysius Thrax, *Art
of Grammar* 636.7
>A grammatical category related to verbs that are used to
>address persons.

Vocative - κλητικός, ή, όν (A.D., *Pron.*) Apollonius Dyscolus,
On Pronouns 6.9
>A grammatical category related to verbs that are used to

address persons.

Vocative (case) - προσαγορευτικός, ή, όν (*Stoic.*) *Stoicorum Veterum Fragmenta / Old Stoic Fragments* 2.61
    Characteristic of nouns that are used to address persons.

Voice - διάθεσις, ή (A.D., *Synt.*) Apollonius Dyscolus, *On Syntax* 210.19
    A grammatical category descriptive of the relationship between the state or action of the verb and the subject.

Vowel - φωνῆεν, τό (S., *Aj.*) Sophocles, *Ajax* 16
    A letter of the alphabet that is not a consonant. In English the main vowels are: a, e, i, o, u.

Vulgar language - ἰδιωτισμός, ό (Phld., *Po.*) Philodemus, *On Poems* 2.71
    The improper or inappropriate use of language or the improper and inappropriate language itself.

Without punctuation - ἀστιγής, ές (St.Byz.) Stephanus
Byzantius (# N/A)
>   When a writing or speech lacks punctuation.

Word, sentence - λόγος, ὁ (A.D., *Synt.*) Apollonius Dyscolus,
On Syntax 3.6
>   An element of speech that contains and conveys meaning.

Wordy (having many words) - πολύλεξις, ι (D.T., *Ars gram.*)
Dionysius Thrax, *Art of Grammar* 25H
>   Characterisic of using big words or too many words.

Writing from right to left & left to right alternatively -
βουστροφηδόν (Paus.) Pausanias 5.17.6
>   A ancient writing pattern in which one line is written from
>   right to left, the next from left to right, etc.

Writing utensil - κάλαμος, ὁ (NT, 3 Ep. Jo.) *3 John* 13
>   A quill, pen, etc.

Writing, scripture - γραφή, ἡ (Pl., *Phdr.*) Plato, *Phaedrus* 274b
>   A text or an object containing composed words usually
>   believed to be sacred (such as a book or scroll).

χειρόγραφα (Notes):

Made in the USA
Lexington, KY
19 September 2014